Motorcycle Journeys Through

The Southwest

Second Edition

Martin C. Berke

Whitehorse Press
Center Conway, New Hampshire

I dedicate this book to my partner, on the road and in life, Pauline. To Tara, Paul, and my newest love in life, Ava. And to my friends and family who, regardless of the miles between us, share, encourage, nurture, and enrich my life.

Interior photography by Pauline Davis and Martin Berke unless otherwise noted.

We recognize that some words, model names and designations mentioned herein are the property of the trademark holder. We use them for identification purposes only.

Whitehorse Press books are also available at discounts in bulk quantity for sales and promotional use. For details about special sales or for a catalog of motorcycling books, videos, and gear write to the publisher:
Whitehorse Press
107 East Conway Road
Center Conway, New Hampshire 03813
Phone: 603-356-6556 or 800-531-1133
E-mail: CustomerService@WhitehorsePress.com
Internet: www.WhitehorsePress.com

ISBN 978-1-884313-66-0

5 4 3 2 1

Printed in the United States of America

Acknowledgments

I want to thank all the people who helped make tens of thousands of miles into a book. They are the open, honest people who shared with me their feelings and their hometowns. In the world today, they are constant reminders and renewers of goodwill.

Contents

Introduction

Hi, Gang. We're off to the Southwest again, a touring goal for every motorcyclist. Many things have changed since the first edition . . . except for the great roads!

Many modern highways evolved from some old frontier path whose inspiration was a well-worn footpath. Such roads may offer the most direct route, but seldom lift the human spirit. *Motorcycle Journeys Through the Southwest* proves that a straight line is not the shortest way to fun.

This book is for you and your motorcycle journeys. It creates destinations and helps you maximize your riding time while exploring the Southwest.

A journey, unlike a trip, is an opportunity for wandering and exploring new territory with all five senses. My intent is to get you going, present choices, and encourage you to venture on your own while sharing the kinship of the open road with routes like Route 66, rivers like the Rio Grande, and railroads like the Durango and Silverton Narrow Gauge.

The "Triple R," one of my favorite configurations, is found wherever road, river, and railroad run in parallel. Pulling the cord on my imaginary whistle when a train passes by usually gets a real toot reply, one of the most seductive sounds to a wanderer. If motorcyclists have an addiction, it is to the setting off, not the arrival.

While this book is not designed to tell you everything—some locals may be reluctant to tell even their mothers about an old mine for fear she'd be digging there the next morning—it will get you on your way. I do not list every bump in the road or even every obvious attraction. This book, however, is written with the special needs of motorcyclists in mind: you'll find comments on out-of-the-way breakfast places, funky attractions, and most of all roads, the smallest narrowest curvy little gray squiggles on all those Interstate maps.

As for the routes, think of them as starting points, giving you the benefit of my knowledge and experience while allowing you to build your own repertoire of favorite journeys. Depending on the time you have available, the kind of terrain you enjoy, and of course, your whim, you will quickly build your own custom journeys through the Southwest.

The terrain of the Southwest can be appreciated any time of year. Ride through Rocky Mountain passes, throwing snowballs in summer; warm your hide in winter on the Sonoran Desert floor, or do both on the same spring day. The book is designed to take you through it all: verdant valleys, still blue waters, majestic purple mountains, brown rolling hills, tan sculptured dunes, rushing white rivers, carved red rock, and twisting blacktop.

Unlike other travel books, *Motorcycle Journeys Through the Southwest* does not always end at a neat political cutoff such as a state line. This book follows the contours of geography and/or cultures. For example, the section "Hanging on the Mogollon Rim" follows the Mogollon Rim from New Mexico through Arizona. "Grand Circle" follows watershed flows and the Colorado River through Utah, Arizona, and Nevada. "West Slope Slalom" explores the west side of the Continental Divide. "Enchantment Land" integrates the tri-cultural State of New Mexico with the desert, mountains, and Rio Grande River. "Bloomin' Desert" ranges from humble Spanish Missions to the bold military missions of Coronado and Cochise, generals and Geronimo, and includes folklore icons of the Wild West like the Earps, Clantons, and Tombstone. "Front Range" flaunts wild, deep canyon rides to the highest paved road in North America, while fording rivers on the east side of the Continental Divide.

The road to Monument Valley gives the traveler a sense of the awesome scale of nature.

For the ultimate in geopolitical travel book defiance, the "2 x Four Corners" section plays within all four states included in this book: Arizona, Colorado, New Mexico, and Utah. That section explores the ruins, legacy, and mysterious disappearance of the thousand-year-old Anasazi ("Ancient Ones" in Hopi) while traveling through contemporary Navajo, Hopi, Ute, and Apache lands. Motorcycle touring is not about following the dotted lines; it's about crisscrossing them.

ORGANIZATION OF THIS BOOK

Motorcycle Journeys Through the Southwest contains two kinds of information: descriptions of the journeys themselves and useful "on the road" information. The journeys described in this book take advantage of the variety of terrain, the vastness of territory, and geographic, cultural, or historical continuity.

As a matter of safety, comfort, and personal preference, I like to establish a base camp or home base. This allows me a more nimble ride without my touring gear and gives me more time to ride by not having to set up or break camp each day. I prefer the environmental immersion of camping, but depending on your budget and personal preference, your choices range from campgrounds to motels, to bed & breakfasts, or dude ranches, dude.

Each "journey" or chapter in this book describes two to five trips. At the beginning of each journey and trip, there's an orientation to the geography and/or history of the area and a description of its home base.

Each journey is made up of several "loops" or "trails;" a home base is located centrally among them. A loop begins and ends at home base and equals a day's ride. I designed a full day of riding for each loop, including unique places, attractions, points of interest, and a way back to home base. The loops themselves average between 150 and 250 miles and encompass tight twisties, open road, scenic vistas, and a place or two to picnic. Variety is the spice of loops. If your style leans toward marathon riding, combine a couple of loops.

"Trails" are open trips, usually a day or two in length, connecting two contiguous areas or chapters. Instead of returning to home base, trails are a pack-your-gear-and-move-to-a-new-home-base-in-the-next-area ride.

Exploring two areas and connecting their home bases through a trail makes for a week's vacation. Exploring a major section of this book will occupy a two-week vacation. Two sections makes for a month's foray, and doing the entire book will keep you in heaven for a quarter of a year.

MAPS

Throughout the book, we've placed map segments to help you find your way. We used the following conventions when making the maps:

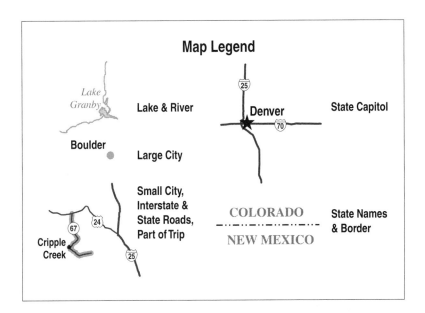

THOUGHTS AND FEEDBACK

"If future generations are to remember us more with gratitude than sorrow, we must achieve more than just the miracles of technology. We must also leave them a glimpse of the world as it was created, not just as it looked when we got through with it." - LBJ

The Grand Canyon is a humbling reminder of how fleeting we are in the scheme of history. This mile-deep canyon unveils 250 million years of geologic history. Each step down from the rim represents 20,000 years of history. Three steps down the trail and you've passed the time we humans appeared on this planet.

Motorcycle Journeys Through the Southwest can always use improving. I am always interested in your opinions. If you have favorite roads to suggest, ideas to make this book more useful, or other helpful hints to offer, please send them along to me, care of the publisher.

Well, enough introductions. Let's go for that "glimpse of the world as it was created." Thanks and keep it between the ditches.

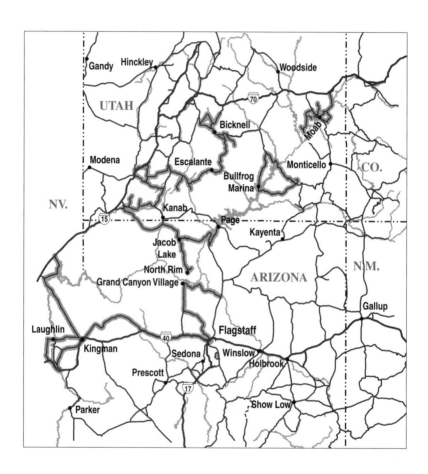

Grand Circle

The Grand Circle offers unsurpassed scenery. With no beginning and no end, and a circumference of roughly 1,300 miles, the Grand Circle is one continuous trail encompassing six national parks, two national monuments, two national recreation areas, four national forests, three major dams, and the two largest man-made lakes in the United States. For backup, numerous state parks, historical sites, and an education in geology await you as well.

The Colorado Plateau, which geologically dominates southeastern Utah, northern Arizona, and western Colorado, features striking colors and rock formations. Erosion is the designer of the region, carving layers of sandstone and limestone into bizarre and awesome shapes. Most of the Colorado Plateau in Utah is desert. Rain and snow are not frequent and that which does fall runs quickly into the Colorado River and Lake Powell.

Plan to remain as long as possible exploring the rugged mountains, fast rivers, and blue lakes against deep red canyon walls. Each place is so unique that it doesn't seem fair that they should be so close together. Each mile of road capitalizes on the beauty and splendor of the region, including a top ten scenic road, Route 12. Did I mention the best ride that Route 66 has to offer?

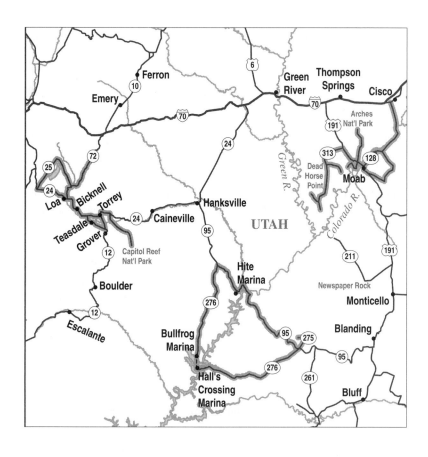

Canyonlands of Utah

Home base for the first two trips of this section is **Dead Horse Point State Park**, (www.utah.com/stateparks/dead_horse.htm, 435-259-2614) an isolated island mesa towering 2,000 feet above the Colorado River, overlooking 5,000 square miles of panoramic spires, pinnacles, and buttes of Utah's **Canyonlands National Park**. While most people strive for **Arches National Park**, (www.nps.gov/arch, 435-719-2299) and understandably so, Dead Horse offers additional conveniences, and is less crowded to boot.

The closest town to Dead Horse is **Moab**, Utah, and it offers all the amenities of a tourist town. The town is home to the **Hollywood Stuntmen's Hall of Fame** (members.aol.com/fdtex/stunt.html, 435-259-7027) and **Eddie McStiffs**, (www.eddiemcstiffs.com, 435-259-beer) one of four brewpubs allowed in Utah, an otherwise dry state.

The Stuntmen's Hall of Fame is the result of dedication and the inspiration of John Hagner. A stuntman for over 20 years, Hagner has doubled for the likes of Robert Mitchum, among others. Like Grumman's Chinese Theater, footprints of famous stunt people and actors adorn the sidewalk outside. Inside the museum is memorabilia from films shot in the Moab area—*Thelma & Louise, Indiana Jones and the Last Crusade,* and many western classics like *Wagon Master* and *The Comancheros*. Costumes, weapons, stunt equipment, and photos depict stuntmen at their best. Daily screenings of memorable stunt scenes make the tour complete.

 THE STORY BEHIND DEAD HORSE POINT

In the late 1800s mustang herds ran wild on the mesas. Dead Horse Point got its name from its use as a natural corral into which the horses were driven. The only escape from the promontory was a narrow 30-yard neck of land controlled by fencing. The mustangs were roped and broken, while the less desirable "broomtails" were left behind to find their own way off the point. The name, according to legend, came from a band of broomtails who for some unknown reason remained on the point and died of thirst while staring at the rushing waters of the Colorado River, 2,000 feet below. ∎

Trip 1   Dead Horse Point to La Sal Mountains Salsa Loop

Distance *185 miles*
Highlights *From the 9,000 foot highs of the La Sal Mountain Loop Road to the lows of the Colorado River at 4,000 feet, with plenty in between*

THE ROUTE FROM DEAD HORSE POINT STATE PARK

Route 313 east to Route 191 south
Route 191 south to Moab, turn left on 300 south
300 south to 2nd right on 400 east
400 east to first left onto Mill Creek Drive
Mill Creek Drive to Spanish Valley Drive
Spanish Valley Drive to left on La Sal Mountain Loop Road (just after Ken's Lake)
La Sal Mountain Loop Road to Route 128 north
Route 128 north to Cisco and turn around
Route 128 south to Route 191 north
Route 191 north to Route 313 west to home base

Spanish Valley Road, which parallels Route 191 south, starts its climb up the La Sal Mountains just after Ken's Lake. The La Sal Mountains are the second largest range in Utah, with Mount Peale rising to an elevation of 12,721 feet.

The La Sal Loop Road reminds you of the way back roads used to be, an old-fashioned ride where riders take responsibility for themselves. Hairpins, 14 percent grades, and blind corners, all without DPW "two-bumps-22-miles-per-hour-for-the-next-3.2-miles-in-third-gear-only-please" signage. Paved the entire way, the road is a scenic ascent into the Manti-La Sal National Forest.

Dotted with meadows, lakes, and trees, with peaks in the 12,000- to 13,000-foot range, the forest is perfect for a refreshing vista picnic after a hot desert ride. The climb begins with piñon and juniper, gives way to oak, then to larger pines and aspen. At the top are spruce and fir. The challenging climb ends with a panoramic view of Castle Valley, a popular filming location for movies and commercials. On the way down the northwest end of the loop, you run into the Colorado River.

Known locally as "The River Road," Route 128 is a dazzling road of colors, light, and shadow, with the Colorado River on one side and sheer red

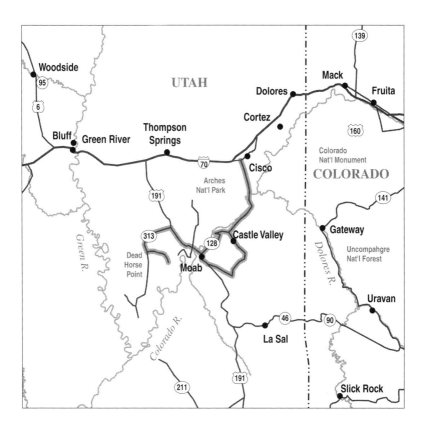

rock cliffs on the other. The Colorado also offers another kind of scenery: rafters and floaters heading downstream to Moab. Don't worry about turning around, the road is a beauty both ways.

By the way, that suspension bridge to nowhere is **Dewey Bridge,** a single-laner that was used until 1986. Now open only to foot traffic, it is on the **National Historic Register.**

There are no facilities in **Cisco,** so fill up in **Moab** before beginning the La Sal Mountain climb. P.S.—The "River Road" is a great alternative to super-slabbing between Moab, Utah, and **Grand Junction,** Colorado.

The way back to Dead Horse Point State Park climbs Seven Mile Canyon from the 4,000-foot floor to the 6,000-foot point. If you're making this trip at night, watch out for the abundant nocturnal wildlife. A herd of deer live on the mesa and twice I had to hit my brakes for eight- and ten-point bucks. Secondly, in late summer and early fall, violent thunderstorms give a dazzling, deadly display of fireworks. Late at night, knowing you're the highest object on the mesa, watching five- and six-second bolts of lightning strike around you is as unnerving as it is exhilarating.

Trip 2 Arches to Canyonlands Loop

Distance *145 miles*

Highlights *Natural wonders in shades of red, green, and blue. Bring water, food, and a good pair of walking shoes.*

THE ROUTE FROM DEAD HORSE POINT STATE PARK

Route 313 east, left at junction (sign to Canyonlands National Park)
Return to Route 313 east
Route 313 east to Route 191 south
Route 191 south to Arches National Park
Return to Route 191 north *
Route 191 north to Route 313 west and home base

* ALTERNATE ROUTE

Route 191 south to Route 279 north and return to US 191 north

Real landscapes at Canyonlands National Park conjure up lots of imaginative images.

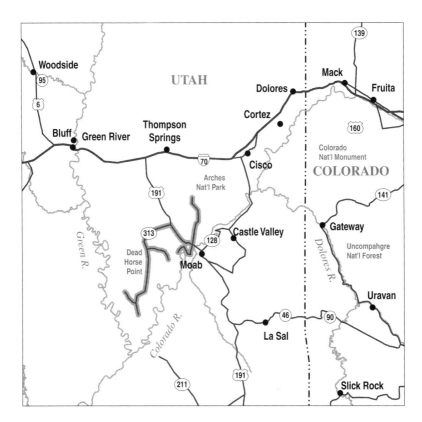

Canyonlands National Park (www.nps.gov/cany, 435-719-2313) is cut into three wedges by the Green River, the Colorado River, and their confluence. This loop visits the **Island in the Sky** region. Island in the Sky got its name because an aerial view shows an island mesa with the only access through a 40-foot narrow neck. Otherwise it's a 2,000-foot drop to the next level. Going down!

Three short hikes (really walks) to Mesa Arch (1/2 mile), Upheaval Dome (1 mile), and Grand View Point Overlook (2 miles) deserve the effort. Mesa Arch is a span of Navajo Sandstone which hangs precariously on the edge of a cliff. Through the arch is a striking view of the La Sal Mountains, 35 miles away. Upheaval Dome is a bit of a mystery. Measuring 1,500 feet deep, the dome doesn't look like a dome at all but a crater that may have been created by the impact of a giant meteor. And Grand View Point offers scenery that stretches a hundred miles across canyon after canyon.

The road itself has less logic than the landscape. The only way I could rationalize the construction was through this imaginary conversation between the engineer and contractor:

You can practice your S-turns at Island in the Sky District of Canyonlands National Park.

"I ordered the 36 miles of asphalt. It will be here next week and we got a real bargain."

"Thirty-six miles! The road I designed only needs 24 miles of construction."

"Twenty-four miles! What are we going to do with the rest, I can't return it."

"I got an idea," said the engineer. "Why don't I just S-turn the s—— out of the road. I can make 24 miles stretch into 36."

"Great idea, let's start a few miles past the visitor center so the muckety-mucks never see it."

The conversation may be imaginary, but the road is real. This is a great road for practicing those S-turns.

Arches National Park (www.nps.gov/arch, 435-719-2299) contains the world's largest concentration of these natural stone openings. There are more than 1,500 arches in the park, ranging in size from a minimum 3-foot opening to 105-foot Landscape Arch. All stages of arch formation and decay are found. Delicate Arch defies comprehension as it stands alone on the brink of a canyon.

The park lies on top of a giant underground salt bed. Thousands of feet thick, it was covered with residue from floods and oceans. Salt liquefies under pressure, resembling molten plastic. Under this pressure, the salt buckled and shifted, thrusting the earth layers upward. Today, the salmon-colored Entrada Sandstone is the visible remains and building materials for the arches. Over time, water and ice entered the fissures of these upheavals and, with wind to scour the loosened rock, dissolved the cementing material away.

With most of the viewing from the road, the only walk of substance is Devil's Garden Trail. For two miles, hike among the fins that form arches, past six other arches, to Double O Arch. The scenic roadway is crowded but has plenty of passing zones.

If these aren't enough sightseeing miles, or if you want to combine all the features of the **Moab**, Utah area into a short 36-mile round tripper, add Route 279 to the agenda. Riding alongside the Colorado River, this road offers arches, dinosaur tracks, mountain climbing and climbers, ancient ruins and petroglyphs, and free primitive camping.

To continue on the Grand Circle, head south from Moab, Utah, to **Hite Marina** at Lake Powell and Trip 3. On the trail to Hite, take a side trip to the Squaw Flats Scenic Byway. Beginning 14 miles north of Monticello, this 35-mile scenic drive runs west, off Route 191, to **Newspaper Rock State Park** (www.utah.com/schmerker/2000/newsrock.htm, 800-635-6622).

Newspaper Rock is an ancient Anazasi petroglyph panel covering a 50-foot high rock face and recording approximately 2,000 years of early human activities. In Navajo the rock is called "Tsé Hané" (rock that tells a story). After Newspaper Rock, the road leads to the Canyonlands' Needles District and its towering red rock canyon.

Trip 3 A Touch of Lake Mead

Distance *176 miles*
Highlights *Canyons, water, desert, and a few accessible Anasazi ruins thrown in. Unless a Mae West is standard issue for your bike, here's an alternate way to see Lake Powell.*

THE ROUTE FROM HITE MARINA CAMPGROUND

Access road to Route 95 west
Route 95 west to Route 276 south
Route 276 south to ferry crossing at Bullfrog Marina. Follow signs to ferry
Route 276 north from ferry terminal at Hall's Crossing
Route 276 north to Route 95 east
Route 95 east to Route 275 north and return
Route 95 west to access road to Hite Marina. Follow signs to the marina

Hite Marina (www.nps.gov/glca/planyourvisit/lake-powell-marinas.htm, 435-684-2457), home base for this loop, is named after **Cass Hite**, an early prospector who made more money ferrying people across the river than digging around it. The ferry and the town of Hite existed until they were flooded by the rising waters of Lake Powell. Now there is free camping on the shore, with plenty of driftwood for fuel, drinking water, bathroom facilities, a gas station, and a convenience store within walking distance, making this one of the better bargain spots.

This loop skirts the northern portion of the lake. Crossing the Dirty Devil River, this road climbs up and around the headwaters of the lake. At one point you've driven ten miles only to be exactly on the shore opposite Hite Marina. Most of the loop is a speed-limit two-laner no-brainer down through Trial Canyon and across the Cane Spring Desert into **Bullfrog Marina.**

The ferry crossing is 15 minutes of prep for a 25-minute ride. Being out to sea for three bucks is like an amusement ride. The ferry runs every two hours on the odd hour from Bullfrog. The even hours are from **Hall's Crossing.** There's always room for a bike, so don't sweat being bumped. Be sure to put the bike on the center stand, as the ferry docks "by feel."

Out of Hall's Crossing, stop at mile marker 68 and park at the pullout on the left-hand side. A hundred-yard stroll up a well-worn foot path to the red cliffs brings an Anasazi ruin into view. It is remarkably preserved for being so close to the road. For those of you who avoided all the other ruins of the

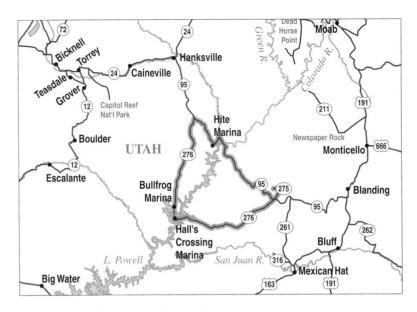

"Ancient Ones," no excuse for a little exploration at this convenient uninhabited location.

Natural Bridges National Monument (www.nps.gov/nabr, 435-692-1234) perched on Cedar Mesa at an elevation of 6,500 feet, is just a short hop past Red House Cliffs next to the Grand Gulch Primitive Area. The difference between a natural bridge and an arch is in the erosion action. An arch is formed by water seeping in and freezing, and wind carrying away debris. Natural bridges are formed by the erosion of running water.

The monument consists of three of the largest natural bridges in North America, each bridge representing a different stage of formation.

Owachomo (meaning "rock mound") is in the late (elderly) stages. A fatal crack may be started already. Sipapu (meaning "the spirit place of emergence upon birth and departure upon death") is an adult or mature bridge. It is 220 feet high, spans 268 feet, is 31 feet wide, and 53 feet thick. The last and youngest is Kachina (named for the rock art symbol Kachina doll or "ghost dancer"). Flood waters in White Canyon continue to work on enlarging Kachina.

Legend has it that Cass Hite was the first white man to discover the bridges while looking for a lost silver mine. Instead of silver, he found the three bridges and named them Congressman, Senator, and President in order of size. The Ute Indians called all natural bridges "Mah-vah-talk-tump" which means "under the horse's belly." The bridges were finally given their Hopi names. Natural Bridges has a primitive 13-site campground if need be.

Trip 4 Capitol Reef to Fish Lake Loop

Distance

162 miles

Highlights

Scenery, curves, hairpins. The landscape ranges from desert to high mountain lakes and meadows.

THE ROUTE FROM CAPITOL REEF NATIONAL PARK

Route 24 west to Route 25 north

Route 25 north to Route 72 north

Route 72 north to Hogan's Pass and turn around

Route 72 south to Route 24 east

Route 24 east to right at sign to Teasdale

Main Street to Route 12 east (sign to Torrey)

Route 12 east to Route 24 east

Route 24 east to Capitol Reef Scenic Drive and return

Capitol Reef National Park was named for its resemblance to the Capitol building in Washington, D.C.

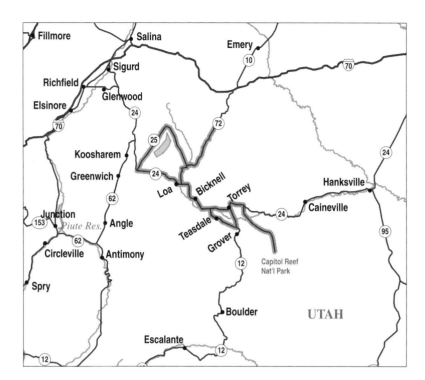

This loop has several potential home bases. If **Capitol Reef National Park** (www.nps.gov/care, 435-425-3791 ext.111) is full, go commercial at **Thousand Lakes RV Park** (www.thousandlakesrvpark.com, 800-355-8995) in Torrey, Utah, for all the conveniences, or go primitive, at 8,900 feet, in **Fish Lake National Forest** (www.fs.fed.us/r4/fishlake, 435-896-9233). **Fish Lake Lodge** (www.fishlake.com, 435-638-1000) has cabins for groups. You can't go wrong with any of the choices.

Capitol Reef National Park is described as "the fantasy of Bryce Canyon and the grandeur of Zion, with more color than either." The park's role is to preserve nearly a quarter-million acres of towering cliffs and eroding landscape, including the Waterpocket Fold.

The water flowing along Route 24 is the Fremont River. Following the Fold, the Fremont winds past the Capitol Dome, named for its resemblance to the Capitol Dome Building in Washington. Just past the Capitol Dome is my favorite waterfall name, Boogie Man Falls. This man-made waterfall is named for the kids who almost drown every year from the undertow. The reef portion of the park's name comes from the pioneers' struggle with the formidable Waterpocket Fold. As with seafarers, they called any barrier to a safe harbor a reef.

THE WRINKLE IN MOTHER NATURE'S LAYER CAKE

The Waterpocket Fold is a giant snaking wrinkle, 100 miles long in the earth's crust, across south central Utah. A survival tool for the plants and pioneers alike, the fold captures thousands of gallons of water each rainfall.

This buckling, created by the upheaval which produced the Colorado Plateau, occurred 65 million years ago when many layers of sedimentary rock, originally horizontal and formed by the great seas and tidal flats, flexed into a huge fold. Looks like the melding of sleeping bag and clothes inside my tent in the morning.   ■

The scenic drive to Capitol Reef Gorge is filled with colors and shapes, mammoth and jagged, on all sides of the narrow band of asphalt which cuts through the heart of the park. Sometimes there is sand at the bottom of dips where washes cross. And we all appreciate sand for its disaster potential.

After Capitol Reef National Park, the first civilization available is in **Torrey,** Utah, a small town of 800 with a couple of gastronomic surprises. Snacking? The **Chuck Wagon General Store** has its own bakery. The multigrain bread and blueberry cheese Danish are superb.

On the road through Fish Lake National Forest are many remote stops. The Wild Bunch holed up and stashed their booty here.

LEGENDS OF FISH LAKE

Fish Lake spawns legends as well as fish. The most intriguing are the legends of Dark Shadow and the buried booty of Butch Cassidy's Wild Bunch. Dark Shadow dreamed that he, his father, Red Cloud, and his sister, Naomee, returned from a camping trip to find Sheena, Dark Shadow's mother, dead in the tipi. The dream upset Dark Shadow so terribly that he couldn't sleep. Hearing of the anguish, a warrior told Dark Shadow to see the Great Medicine Man, who could break the spell of the dream.

Upon hearing the dream, the Medicine Man said, "To break the spell, you must catch a mackinaw fish from the Lake and cut out its heart. Wrap the heart in the skin of a porcupine and bury it in a grove of aspen. This all must be done under a full moon."

It was almost the time of a full moon, so Dark Shadow had little time to waste. He hunted and skinned a porcupine, but catching a mackinaw trout was a difficult and seldom-achieved feat. He fished for several hours and was on the brink of giving up when he caught the great fish.

With little of the full moon left, he raced up the mountainside and buried the fish in a hole he had already prepared. The spell was broken. Even today, although the tribe no longer exists, the symbol of Dark Shadow's love for his mother is evident. In autumn, on the hillside across from the lodge, enclosed in a grove of golden aspens, where Dark Shadow buried the charm, is a heart-shaped grove of ruby-red leaves.

The Wild Bunch legend starts on June 2, 1899 when the Wild Bunch robbed the Union Pacific Flyer of $30,000 in gold coins, then fled from Wyoming to Hole in the Wall country in Wayne County, the site of Fish Lake. Evidence seems to indicate that the buried booty was stashed in a small valley overlooking Fish Lake, where the waters of the lake flowed through. They never returned to claim it. That means the loot is still buried somewhere along the Owl Hoot Trail.   ■

After strapping on the feedbag, hit the road for Fish Lake National Forest. Route 24 from Torrey to Loa cuts through Boulder Mountain on the left and Thousand Lakes Mountain on the right. Funny, the red cliffs and bald tops of Thousand Lakes and the green lush top of Boulder Mountain made me wonder how they got their names.

Asking an old timer that very question, I got, "Well it's another example of the government at work. The surveyors had their maps upside down when naming the area because the lakes are on Boulder Mountain and Thousand Lakes is a dry red-rock formation."

The scenic drive through Fish Lake National Forest climbs to over 9,000 feet, from sage brush to high mountain aspen groves, cooling off everything except the ride. The ride gets hotter as the curves climb. Nestled in the steep-sided basin, the glistening blue waters of Fish Lake finally appear. If the weather cooperates, camping is National Forest Service pricing. The Fish Lake Lodge offers amenities not usually found in the wild, including rustic and modern cabins in a motel price range. Breakfast, lunch, and dinner are available too.

Looking to steal a view? The lookout at Hogan Pass is Fort Knox. From this overlook you can see most of southeastern Utah. From the red buttes of Cathedral Valley to the broad rise of the San Rafael Swell, look northeastward over Molly's Castle and the Flat Tops to the Book Cliffs and the La Sal

Riding the splendid Capitol Reef National Park.

EDDIE McSTIFFS

Eddie McStiffs serves up great pizzas and southwestern food. The Burrito Mulege (moo-la-HEY), named after one of my favorite little Mexican towns on the Baja, is especially tasty. Even more tasty are the award-winning beers brewed on the premises. Among the more exotic are Blueberry Wheat, a hint of blueberry mixed with stout, and Amber Ale, copper colored and rich in flavor because of the imported British Carastan malt. There are others named Spruce, Passion Fruit (better than the name suggests), Raspberry Wheat, and Cream Ale. Three-ounce samplers are available. If you're driving, Eddie's offers their own root beer, brewed using Quillaia (South American tree derivative) and a blend of eight different roots.   ■

Mountains. To the southeast, Caineville Mesas and Factory Butte establish foreground for the Henry Mountains. The Henry Mountains are another example of "whoever has the pen, rules". Said to be the last surveyed mountain range in the United States, the Spanish had been mining those mountains 150 years before the U.S. "found" them.

Grand Staircase

Nearly two billion years of the earth's history is revealed from the top of the Markagunt Plateau to the bottom of the Grand Canyon. The sequence of colorful eroded rock layers is called the Grand Staircase. The staircase begins at 10,300 feet with the pink cliffs of **Cedar Breaks National Monument,** capped with bristle cone pines, the oldest living things on earth. Stepping down to the Paunsaugunt Plateau-Bryce National Park, a red rock canyon of spires, spindles, and sheer cliffs just below the eastern edge of the Paunsaugunt Plateau—12 huge bowls sink 1,000 feet into the earth, exposing layer upon layer of colored stone. Fifteen million years of erosion created the montage that is **Bryce Canyon.**

Farther down the staircase, the Virgin River carved the white cliffs of **Zion National Park** from what was once wind-deposited sand dunes. Within the park, the topography ranges from a towering 8,000 feet to 3,700 feet at the bottom.

The last step is a doozy. At the base of the staircase, 8,000 feet below Cedar Breaks, is the greatest demonstration of nature's power. The Colorado River has cut through the Kaibab Plateau in multi-colored layers to reach the dark rocks of the Grand Canyon's inner gorge.

The Grand Parade at the grand entrance to Kodachrome Basin State Park is a welcoming site for home base.

Trip 5 The First Step (Bryce National Park)

Distance *140 miles*

Highlights *One of the top ten scenic roads in the United States. Plan on two days, one to ride to and explore Kodachrome Basin and one to revel in Bryce Canyon.*

THE ROUTE FROM CAPITOL REEF NATIONAL PARK

Route 24 west from Capitol Reef National Reef Park to Route 12 west

Route 12 west to left at Cannonville (sign to Kodachrome Basin State Park)

Return to Route 12 west to Route 63 south

Route 63 south till end and return Route 12 east

Route 12 east to right at Cannonville (sign to Kodachrome Basin State Park) and home base

Hoodoos at Bryce Canyon National Park allow you to play "who do dat" resemble.

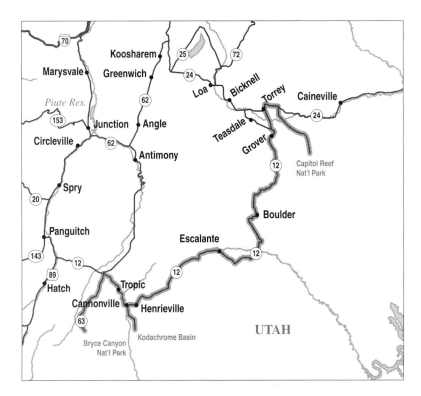

At the end of this step, make **Kodachrome Basin State Park** (www.utah-.com/stateparks/kodachrome.htm, 435-679-8562) your home base for the exploration of **Bryce Canyon National Park.** This logistical choice gives you two opportunities to discover the extraordinary and varied landscapes of both parks without the hustle and bustle of national parkdom. Kodachrome Basin is a little-known spot with 24 private campsites, modern facilities, showers, and supplied firewood.

In addition to the amenities, the campground is situated deep in a multi-colored basin. Without car noise to distract or light pollution to obstruct, it offers one of the finer views of our galaxy, the Milky Way. Like a silver river across the sky, depending on the moonshine, the show is so close, it will touch you, even though you can't touch it.

Kodachrome Basin has the added advantage of its own short hikes to the tops and edges of land formations for uncrowded, up close views of mother nature's canvas and palette. The National Geographic Society aptly named it Kodachrome Basin, for it challenges the photographer to capture the red rock, white limestone, and blue sky. The beauty of these colored rock formations shifts with your imagination and the time of day.

Geologists feel the area was once similar to what **Yellowstone National Park** is today (and we can glimpse what Yellowstone will be tomorrow, when geothermally dead from the encroachment of civilization). The spires or chimneys were geysers and springs that filled with sediment and resisted the erosion of the softer Entrada sandstone surrounding them. Check out the "Grand Parade" at the entrance to Kodachrome around sundown. Kodachrome Basin's seclusion gives it a more intimate quality than Bryce and its 5,700-foot elevation makes it warmer than Bryce's 8,000 feet. The extra 40-mile round trip from Kodachrome Basin is also a bonus.

Getting to Kodachrome Basin means one of the most scenic rides in the United States, Utah Route 12. Not paved until 1986, the first part of the ride enters **Dixie National Forest** by climbing and winding its way over 9,400-foot Boulder Mountain. The overlook at the summit gives one of the more expanded views of the Waterpocket Fold as it runs through **Capitol Reef National Park**. From here, it's downhill through Boulder.

If you're a dirt biker, try the 66-mile Burr Trail running from this frontier town across the Waterpocket Fold to **Bullfrog Marina** on Lake Powell. A 4-wheel drive road, it is not for the faint of heart or scooter. Stop at the **Burr Trail Cafe** (www.burrtrailoutpost.com, 435-335-7565) for a local assessment, some down-home cooking, and frontier humor.

Route 12, after **Boulder,** gets real squiggly and colorful. Climbing the Kaiparowits Plateau, scaling red, white, and sandal colored terrain, then dropping into Escalante River Canyon, crossing the Escalante River on a one-lane bridge, and crossing convoluted countryside, it's a slow, awesome ride of geologic variety and concentration. Did I mention a narrow mesa-top road with 500-foot cliffs falling off both sides? Not a place to get the wobblies.

Down and past **Escalante** and its petrified forest, re-enter Dixie National Forest and begin the ascent over the Table Cliffs Plateau. Coming off the plateau, breeze through **Henrieville** toward **Cannonville** and Kodachrome Basin State Park.

Bryce Canyon National Park (www.nps.gov/brca, 435-834-5322) is a perfect backdrop for a science fiction movie. Named for Ebenezer Bryce, a pioneer, the park is a surreal landscape of figures, silhouettes, and characters by the thousands (called hoodoos). It's fun to play "hoodoos" here—"who do" that resemble?

The range of colors in the limestone layers at Bryce Canyon seems endless. Limestone in its pure form is white. Small amounts of iron oxidizes or rusts into the yellow-reds-brown ranges of color. Manganese oxides cause the blue and purple. It's like being in Giant Creamsicle Land.

Don't forget Fairyland Canyon on the way out of Bryce.

The Paiute have a different theory on the origins of Bryce and its color-ation. According to Indian Dick in 1936, "Before there were any Indians, The Legend People, To-when-an-ung-wa lived in that place . . . Because they were bad, Coyote turned them all into rocks. You can see them in that place now; some standing in rows; some sitting down; some holding onto others. You can see their faces, with paint on them just as they were before they became rocks . . . The name of that place is Agka-ku-wass-a-wits (Red Painted Faces)."

Take a hike, it's the only way to immerse yourself in the hoodoos of pink, red, and orange, blended with white, gray, and cream. Bits of lavender, yellow, and brown round out the array. There are 23 clearly marked trails to choose from, ranging from a half hour walk to a day . . . or night. Park rangers offer moonlight hikes for exploring the unpolluted night sky. The air is so clean it is possible to see up to 200 miles.

When asked to describe his namesake maze-like canyon, Ebenezer Bryce declared, "It's a hell of a place to lose a cow."

Plan on spending the whole day riding the 32-mile round-trip scenic drive. Lookout after lookout, hoodoo after hoodoo, hour after hour in an ever-changing landscape makes for lingering. Don't forget to view Fairyland Canyon, past the entrance station, on your way out. So many people zoom right by it because they think they have left the park. It's one of the more captivating vistas.

Bryce is one of the more intimate national parks. Not massive, deliberate, or obvious, like a herd of buffalo, Bryce has a delicacy more like a ballerina.

Trip 6 A Hop and a Skip (Cedar Breaks, Zion)

Distance *195 miles*
Highlights *Ride from the top of Brian Head, at 11,307 to the bottom of Zion at 3,700 feet. Cool, treed, and squiggly to massive, towering, and tunneled*

THE ROUTE FROM KODACHROME BASIN STATE PARK

Kodachrome Basin State Park to Route 12 west

Route 12 west to Route 89 north

Route 89 north to Route 143 west

Route 143 west to Route 148 south

Route 148 south to junction of Route 14. Turn around

Route 148 north to Route 143 west

Route 143 west to Route 130 south (follow signs in Parowan to Enoch and
   Cedar City)

Route 130 south to Route 14 east

Route 14 east to Route 89 south

Route 89 south to Route 9 west

Route 9 west to Zion National Park

Cedar Breaks National Park is where the earth takes a dramatic break away from the Markagunt Plateau.

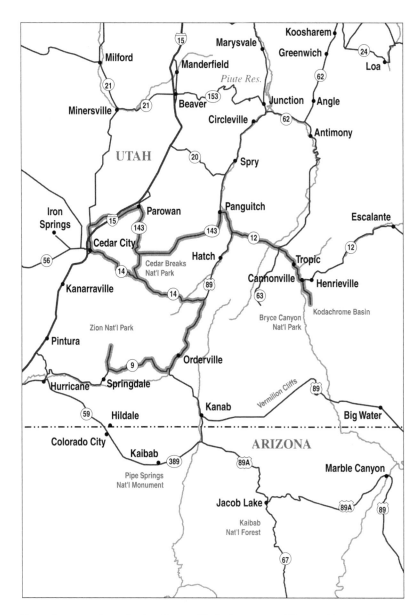

Just when you thought that Bryce, Kodachrome, and Route 12 east of Bryce were the prettiest places in the United States, along comes **Red Canyon**. Sometimes referred to as "Little Bryce," Red Canyon has two tunnels with enough curves and S-turns to make you see red.

A little bit of Texas in Utah. The homemade Tollie's sauce is A-1 in my book.

Speaking of redeye, the next town, **Panguitch,** Utah (Paiute for "Big Fish"), is where Butch Cassidy met his mother for the last time, awwwh. If you want a bite to eat, and your timing is right, the **Cowboy's Smokehouse** (435-676-8030), is a little bit of Texas in Utah. Not only will they fill the belly with their own smoked meats and turkey, but also provide a history lesson on the range origins of smoked brisket, spare ribs, pinto beans (frijoles), and fruit cobblers. Don't forget "Tollie's Sauce," first concocted on the rolling plains of Texas and used to liven up whatever was for dinner. Most often the cowhand was faced with armadillo, rabbit, squirrel, javelina, or rattlesnake. This sauce made even the driest meats savory. Originally made from saddlebag ingredients, it's now a culinary art form. The homemade Tollie's Sauce at the Cowboy's Smokehouse is A-1 in my book.

➡ TUNNEL VISION

Driving through the mile-long east tunnel is an eerie experience. Take off those sunglasses. If you're traveling west, stop at the ranger booth and ask to be last in line when they perform escort service for the RVs. The escort service stops the two-way traffic for the larger vehicles to ride down the middle of the tunnel. I know that may sound opposite to where you wannabe, but being last allows a real slow drive past chiseled granite windows to some amazing views. Don't tell them I told you. ■

Route 143 begins the steady, steep 32-mile ascent to **Cedar Breaks National Park** (www.nps.gov/cebr, 435-586-0787), a circle of painted cliffs forming a huge amphitheater of colorful eroded rock. Over 2,500 feet from top to bottom, it's deep enough to stack 16 Statues of Liberty. Similar to Bryce in coloring, Cedar Breaks was erroneously named by early settlers who mistook the juniper trees for cedars, and for the Badlands that break

Navajo Lake, formed thousands of years ago, still has no outlet.

Crossing the Virgin River on the Emerald Pools hike at Zion National Park. Hope you've got waterwings.

away from the Markagunt Plateau forming the amphitheater. The Cedar Breaks wildflower show starts as soon as the snow melts and peaks during July and early August. The monument contains stands of pine, spruce, fir, quaking aspen, and bristlecone pines, which live for 15,000 years. If we could only get valve adjustments to last that long.

If you're not cool enough at the 10,350 foot mark, take a ride up **Brian Head** at 11,307 feet. A relatively easy gravel road gives way to a 360-degree view spanning Cedar Breaks, Brian Head ski resort, and the **Dixie National Forest.**

From Brian Head, descend Parowan Canyon to **Parowan**. A little side trip of interest before hitting Parowan is Vermilion Castle, a rock formation near a National Forest Service campground of the same name.

The return trip on Route 14 climbs through steep-walled Cedar Canyon. With lots of sharp curves, the road travels best going east from 5,500-foot **Cedar City** over the 10,500-foot plateau. The road is only open four months a year, so grab it after May or before October.

Navajo Lake was originally formed when lava flowed over the east end of the valley. After thousands of years the lake still has no outlets. Water leaves the valley through numerous sink holes and reappears at Cascade Falls, into the Virgin River and on into **Zion National Park**.

Route 9 is a steady climb to Zion National Park (www.nps.gov/zion, 435-772-0170) at 8,000 feet, and then down into Zion Canyon at 3,700. The topography of the park varies from pine and fir-covered slopes to waterfalls leading to verdant Virgin River-fed banks and spring-fed hanging gardens. Originally named Mukuntuweap when designated as a national park in 1909, Zion is Mother Nature's sculpture garden on a massive scale. The monolithic masterpieces loom along both sides of the park road. The Paiute called Zion the "Land of the Sleeping Rainbow" because of the striped stone formations found throughout the park. They're especially evident along the eastern end of the park before the east tunnel.

The switchback descent, coming out of the mile-long east tunnel, emphasizes a unique feature of Zion. Unlike Cedar Breaks, Bryce, or Grand Canyon, Zion is enjoyed from the bottom up. Immersing yourself in its majesty is definitely neck-breaking. Highlights of Zion are the one-mile (45-minute) hike to Canyon Overlook, just east of the big tunnel, the three-mile (two hour) hike to the Emerald Pools, and the eight-mile (seven hour) hike to Observation Point, with sweeping views of Zion Canyon. Don't cheat yourself by doing only a drive-by.

Zion Canyon is also home base for the end of this day's trail. Section D of Watchman Campground is a quiet tent-only section on the Virgin River and a peaceful place to settle in for a couple of days' exploration. It's only two miles to the grocery store, state store, and restaurants in Springdale.

Trip 7 Jump off the Huge Last Step (North Rim)

Distance *189 miles*

Highlights *A spectacular trip from the bottom of Zion Canyon to the last step of the Grand Staircase and the edge of the North Rim of the Grand Canyon*

THE ROUTE FROM ZION NATIONAL PARK

Route 9 west to right on Kolob Terrace Road (sign to Kolob Reservoir)
Return to Route 9 west to Route 59 east. Turns into Arizona 389 east
Route 389 east to Route 89A south
Route 89A south to Route 67 south. Turn around or fall off the Last Step

The Grand Canyon, viewed from its north rim, is a much more secluded take on one of the seven wonders of the world.

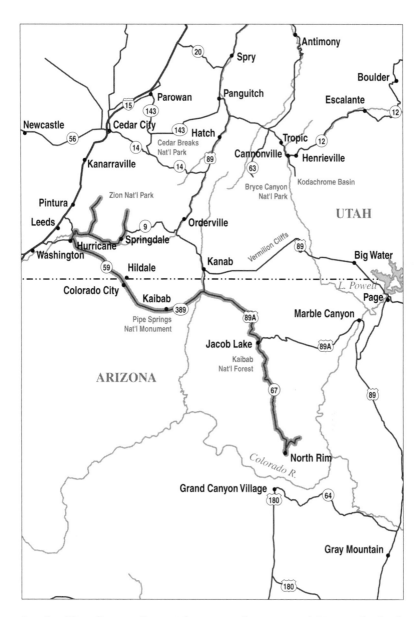

Leaving Zion Canyon, Route 9 becomes a flat open road. You might think the best is behind you, but the road to Kolob Reservoir will change your mind. From about 4,000 feet, this 20 miles of scenic sidewinder climbs 6,000 feet to the 10,000-foot west side of **Zion National Park.**

Back out on Route 9, passing through towns named **Virgin** and **Hurricane,** your ride will parallel the carver of Zion, the Virgin River. From Hurricane, Route 59 climbs the Uinkaret Plateau and rides beside the Vermilion Cliffs. Then down and up the Kaibab Plateau.

On the way to the **North Rim of the Grand Canyon** is **Pipe Spring National Monument** (www.nps.gov/pisp, 928-643-7105). It's a small commemoration of the Native Americans, early explorers, and pioneers who settled this piece of the west. Pipe Springs contains one of the few natural springs on the Kaibab Plateau. The fort, built in the 1870s, was the first historic structure in the National Park System.

Riding to the north rim of the Grand Canyon is a straight, fast, cool climb through tall stands of aspen and pine, across lush meadows of the **Kaibab National Forest** at 8,000 feet. More pristine and forested, the north rim sports an abundance of wildlife, far more than the arid, populated south rim. With one-tenth the visitors of the south rim, this is a more intimate approach to the Grand Canyon. Consider yourself lucky to be the one out of ten visitors who sees the "undiscovered" side.

They come by plane, road, mule, and motorcycle to see the Grand Canyon . . .

. . . and they come by choo-choo, too.

Facilities are more limited on the north rim and close by mid-October. Stay at the National Forest Service's **DeMotte Campground** (928-643-7395), 12 miles outside the park entrance. Lower in cost, smaller in number, yet larger individually, the Demotte sites are preferable to the crowded **North Rim Campground.** Besides, the extra 32 miles to and from the park are beautiful, with herds of deer and flocks (or is that shots) of wild turkeys.

Within the park, ride to **Walhalla Point.** A better name would be Valhalla Drive. Twenty-one miles of curves, lined with aspens, on a narrow two-laner that resembles a New England country lane.

The **Kaibab Lodge,** with its huge glass windows, offers some of the most memorable views in the park. An outdoor patio overlooks the Canadian Life Zone ecology, changing colors faster than a teenager's mood ring, from tranquil shadows to dramatic afternoon thunderstorms.

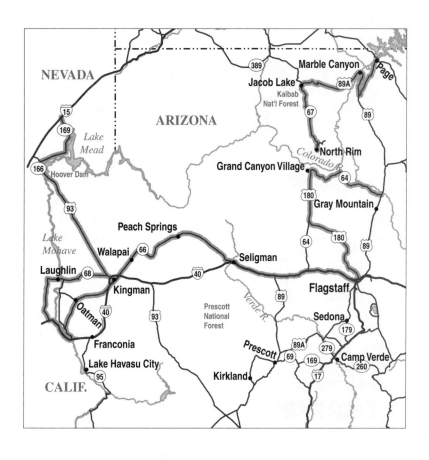

Grand Dams of the Colorado River

From the North Rim of the Grand Canyon, there are two routes to choose. The first goes to **Glen Canyon Dam** and Lake Powell, shortening the Grand Circle by going northwest to Zion Canyon or east to the "2 x Four Corners" section.

The other choice retraces Trip 7 to **Virgin** and picks up Interstate 15 west to Trip 9. This trail then closes the Grand Circle along Route 66 to **Flagstaff** via Trip 10, followed by Trip 11.

Only Laughlin, Nevada, would have a real one-armed bandit.

Trip 8 Grand Canyon to Glen Canyon (Dam) Trail

Distance *124 miles*

Highlights *Descend from a chilly 8,000 feet to a hot 4,800 feet. Riding below Vermilion Cliffs, through Marble Canyon, to Lee Ferry, across Navajo Bridge, up Echo Cliffs, over Glen Canyon Dam, and beside Lake Powell. Home base is Wahweap Campground.*

THE ROUTE FROM THE NORTH RIM OF THE GRAND CANYON

Route 67 north to Route 89 A south

Route 89 A south to Route 89 north

This is a short scenic ride full of natural and man-made structures to enjoy. Crossing the Kaibab Mountains and coming off the Kaibab Plateau are lots of curves and a corkscrew onto House Rock Valley, then a straight desert run below the eye-catching Vermilion Cliffs. Cliff Dwellers is an oasis named after the original trading post built into the rock formations in the early 1900s. The original trading post is a quarter-mile past the new one.

Lake Powell, formed by the Glen Canyon Dam, has a 1986-mile shoreline.

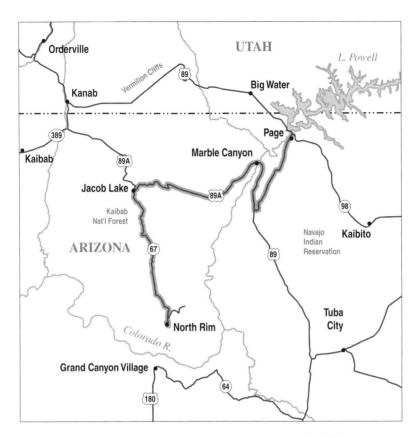

Marble Canyon features brilliant crayon-colored cliffs, appearing washed out lemon in the morning and fiery orange, lipstick red, and deep magenta in the late afternoon. Take the short side trip, off Route 89A, at Marble Canyon to **Lee's Ferry,** established in 1865 as the only crossing of the Colorado River for hundreds of miles. Overturned and lost downstream in 1928, it never reopened because the 500-foot-high Navajo Bridge was finished the following year.

The **Lee's Ferry Campground** in the National Recreation Area, down river from Glen Canyon Dam, is the launch point for rafting and kayaking the Colorado River. The Colorado River drops 2,000 feet during the passage and runs through 160 major rapids.

Rapids are caused by debris from side tributaries which constrict the river flow. When the average depth drops from 35 feet to just a few inches, the water speed increases from 4-5 mph to over 12 mph. Rapids are measured on a scale of one, a small riffle, to 10, the maximum a river-runner will attempt. Just below Lee Ferry is Hermit Rapid, rated a 9. It's a hell of a start.

The day I was there, a six-raft party was departing for the 18-day run through the Grand Canyon. I couldn't help but notice the pallet load of beer in their lined-up provisions. At 95 degrees Fahrenheit, my curiosity got the better of me.

"Are you bringing a fridge with you?" I asked. Someone looked up, knowing exactly what provoked the question, and replied, "We'll let nature do it for us." The water, released from the bottom of 560-foot Glen Canyon Dam, is a constant 45 degrees Fahrenheit. Although I prefer my cool ones at 42 degrees, I'm always amazed at how nature provides.

On the other side of Glen Canyon Dam is the Page/Lake Powell (www.lakepowell.com, 888-896-3829) area. The second largest man-made reservoir in the world has 1,986 miles of shoreline (more than the entire Pacific coast of the United States), five marinas spaced 50 miles apart, and numerous shoreline campgrounds. The National Park Service calls this "a dramatic example of the combination of one of nature's most inspiring settings and one of man's most ambitious projects." For an alternative opinion, read Edward Abbee's "Desert Solitaire."

Page, begun as a construction camp for Glen Canyon Dam, is the gateway to Lake Powell. Sitting on Manson Mesa, it has a perfect view of the lake. Lake Powell's Wahweap Marina and Campground is a large National Recreation Area complex below Page on the shores of the red rock, blue water lake. With the water at 75 degrees Fahrenheit and days between 85 and

---

➡ SIZE MATTERS

The Glen Canyon Bridge is the second highest steel arch bridge in the world. Before it opened on February 20, 1959, the trip from one side of the canyon to the other was 197 miles. The Glen Canyon Dam and its power plant required 5.1 million cubic yards of concrete, poured round the clock for three years, to complete. The dam's crest is 1,560 feet long. It sits on top of 710 feet of bedrock and is 583 feet above the original river channel. At its full pool capacity Lake Powell holds 27 million acre-feet of water 560 feet deep at the dam. It took 17 years to completely fill the lake and what was started on March 13, 1963 was achieved on June 27, 1980. The dam backs up the Colorado River for almost 200 miles to Hite Marina in Utah (imagine how much bran it would take to relieve this problem). For a discussion of Hite Marina see Trip 3.   ■

Oatman is a lively ghost town on Route 66. The burros still visit Main Street daily.

90 degrees during late September, this is an excellent destination for a late gasp of summer's breath.

Swimming at the Coves is a unique experience. The flooding of Glen Canyon enables you to step off 30- and 40-foot cliffs into 500-foot waters. If that's a little steep you can wade a few feet into the water and swim off the ledge. Looking under water while swimming the edge of a canyon is a freaky experience. You can even swim up a canyon from the Coves. How steep is the edge you swam off? Check out the river side of the dam!

Trip 9 Hoover Dam to Davis Dam Trail

Distance *173 miles*
Highlights *Curvy desert road (surprise), dams, lakes, and high stakes*

THE ROUTE FROM INTERSTATE 15

From Interstate 15, take exit 93 onto Nevada Route 169 south

Route 169 south to Route 167 south (Northshore Scenic Drive)

Route 167 south to Route 147 south

Route 147 south to Route 166 east (Lakeshore Drive and signs to Hoover Dam)

Route 166 east to Route 93 south

Route 93 south to Route 68 west

Route 68 west (signs to Davis Dam) to Katherine Drive (sign to campground and Lake Mead National Recreation Area)

Hoover Dam! At Boulder City, Nevada.

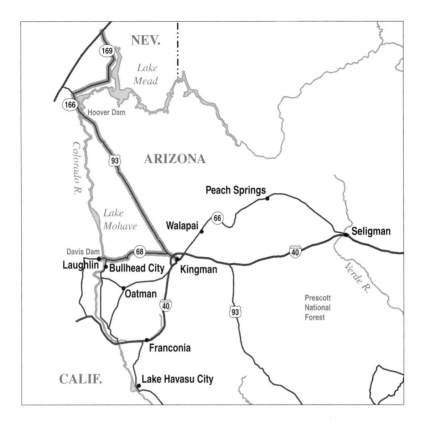

Hoover Dam (www.usbr.gov/lc/hooverdam, 702-494-2302), completed in 1935, turned the turbulent Colorado River into the still waters of Lake Mead (www.nps.gov/lame, 702-293-8990). More than 5,000 people worked day and night for five years to complete the dam. This gigantic 726-foot concrete structure built between the walls of Black Canyon was the highest dam ever built at the time. Lake Mead, twice the size of Rhode Island, is 110 miles long and feeds municipal and industrial water to Los Angeles, San Diego, and other cities in the Southwest.

The Northshore and Lakeshore Drives, encompassing a number of routes that mirror the Lake Mead shoreline, create a challenging desert trail. If you get tired or hot, spur roads lead to campgrounds and swimming areas. All areas are paved and have facilities.

At Hoover Dam you have a choice of heading to **Kingman** via loop directions or returning to **Boulder City** and a straight shot down Route 95 to Route 163 east to **Davis Dam**. Dealer's choice, which seems appropriate, for on the Nevada side of Davis Dam is Laughlin, a suburban Las Vegas on the Colorado River.

Trip 10   Grand Dame Trail (Route 66)

Distance *225 miles*

Highlights *Nostalgia, curves, mountains, a live ghost town, and highways to high country of the San Francisco Peaks*

THE ROUTE FROM DAVIS DAM

Route 68 west to Nevada Route 163 west (over Davis Dam)

Route 163 west to Needles Highway (California) south

Needles Highway to Route 95 south (signs to Golden Shores and Topock, Arizona)

Route 95 south to Route 66 east. * It's a 170-degree merge from the left at Golden Shores

Route 66 east to Frontage Road across Interstate 40 into Kingman

Reunite with Route 66 east to Interstate 40 at Seligman

Interstate 40 to Business 40 (Route 66) in Flagstaff

* ALTERNATE ROUTE

Stay on Route 95 south for Lake Havasu City, the London Bridge, and Lake Havasu beaches in the winter. Return to Route 66 east

The Grand Dame of U.S. roads, Route 66 conjures up a life on the road.

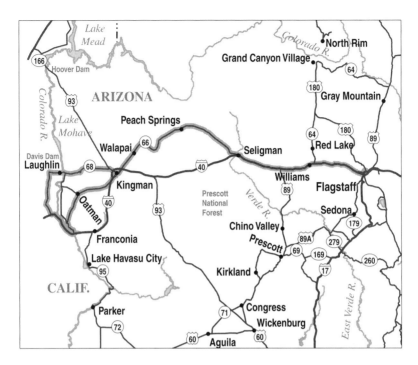

The Nevada ride to **Needles,** California, follows the Colorado River south. With the Dead Mountains to the west and the Mojave Mountains to the east, this tri-state valley ride is picture perfect. Stop at **Chic's Cafe** (760-326-4838), opposite the old Santa Fe Railroad station, for a warm hello and great gourmet coffee and Cajun food daily.

In **Golden Shores,** Route 66 merges with Route 95. Beginning the longest remaining stretch of the road John Steinbeck called "Mother Road," Route 66 heads east for 160 miles. Originally the main east/west corridor, Route 66 connected Chicago with Santa Monica, California. A half-million people migrated from the dust bowl states to fertile California fields in the 1930s on Route 66. Carrying all their worldly possessions in Model A and Model T Fords, these migrants feared the Kingman to Needles portion of Route 66 through the Black Mountains, often hiring locals to drive their cars in the cool of the evening before crossing the Colorado River and entering the Mojave Desert on their journey west.

Route 66 squiggles and dips across the desert floor and slowly rises into the Mojave Mountains. With little signage, it's easy to get above the 45 mph speed limit. Old Route 66 throws a few curves at the unsuspecting, 15 to 25 mph curves to be exact. The climb into the Black Mountains comes fast and furious, all the way to the living ghost town of **Oatman.**

Yes, the Oatman Hotel is where Clark Gable and Carol Lombard honeymooned.

Oatman was named for a migrating pioneer family who was massacred by Tonto-Apache Indians in 1851. Born in 1906 as a tent camp for gold mining, Oatman produced 1.8 million ounces of gold but nearly died when gold became a nonessential material in World War II. The town itself is well preserved—the **Oatman Hotel** (928-768-4408) is on the National Register of Historic Buildings. Check out the dance floor environs and the room where Clark Gable and Carol Lombard honeymooned. It also serves as local hangout for a cast of characters, literally and figuratively. Mornings bring the inhabitants to the hotel for coffee and conversation. On weekends gunfights are staged in the streets. It's real tough to tell the actors from the residents. Movie makers have used Oatman and its setting for such movies as *How the West was Won, Foxfire,* and *Edge of Eternity.*

Every day, wild burros enter the town to be fed by the tourists. Their ancestors were used for mining and freight hauling, but they were released into the wild as people abandoned Oatman. Today, they arrive daily around 10:30 a.m. Buy some alfalfa feed and enjoy the show. If you enjoy stable smells, hang around after the feed, or visit on Labor Day for the annual International Burro Biscuit Tossing.

From Oatman, Route 66 continues its narrow, snaky, 20 mph curves through the Black Mountains, up and over Sitgreaves Pass at 3,652 feet and into **Kingman.** In downtown Kingman, Route 66 is named Andy Devine Avenue after the actor best known for his role as Jingles in the 1950s TV western weekly, "Wild Bill Hickock."

Take a short side trip to the ghost town of **Chloride,** twenty minutes northwest of Kingman on Route 93 and four miles east on Route 62 (the shortest U.S. designated highway in the country). Besides being a more subdued tourist town than Oatman, the old-timers hanging out on the porches give Chloride a lot more character.

Next to the saloon hangs a sign stating "Judge Jim Beam, only law west of the Cerbats." Strolling up to the old-timer I asked, "When did Judge Jim Beam live here?" A little gleam in his eye told me I'd been suckered. "He still rules here," he said, taking a swig from his coffee cup. Then I realized he was talking about the bourbon and I was thinking of Judge Roy Bean.

Just outside of Chloride are artist Roy Purcell's giant cliff murals, "The Journey; images from an inward search for Self." Originally painted in the early 1960s, they were recently restored by Purcell himself in the early 1990s.

Speaking of journeys, although the reality is a straight, flat run with an occasional dip to Interstate 40 and **Flagstaff,** Route 66 from Kingman to **Seligman** is a romance of the mind. Try humming a few bars of Bobby Troup's "(Get your Kicks on) Route 66." Re-enact the TV series that popularized "hitting the road" for a generation.

Here's the shortest highway in the U.S. Four miles to nowhere.

Trip 11   Grand Views of the Grand Canyon (South Rim)

Distance *300 miles*

Highlights *This loop is a two- or three-day affair, depending on how awestruck you are by the views, how long you are off the steed, and how enthused you are about geology, history, and anthropology. Three days is a must if you want to hike the canyon.*

THE ROUTE FROM FLAGSTAFF

Route 180 north (follow signs through Flagstaff) merges Route 64 east

Route 64 east to Route 89 north or south, depending on the next region you choose to explore

Route 180 north out of Flagstaff starts off alpine and pine-lined. Curves dissipate to a straight, flat 50 miles after the San Francisco Peaks which tower over Flagstaff.

The **Grand Canyon** (www.nps.gov/grca, 928-638-7888) being one of the Seven Natural Wonders of the World, attracts visitors worldwide. Driving through on a day ride shows you all the trappings of that many people. Traffic, full viewpoint parking lots, cafeterias, lodges, high prices, and a crowded rim walk trail reminiscent of the old Star Trek episode where the planet couldn't hold another person. How busy are the restaurants? The steak house in the Bright Angel Lodge gave me a handwritten wine list on a napkin!

Stop at the visitor center to get oriented, with information and videotape shows on the hour. Common questions asked by visitors: How come the Anasazi live in ruins? Why did they build their houses so far from the freeway?

If you plan to stay overnight, reservations are a must for the lodges, and can be made for **Mather Campground. Desert View Campground** is first come, first serve. Everything fills up by 10 a.m. in the high season! Staying overnight allows you to hike below the rim, then a whole new world opens up.

Leave the commercial world behind and the grandeur unfolds. The Grand Canyon is 277 miles long and 10 miles wide, and the Colorado River has so far cut a swath one mile deep in a low rounded mountain called Kaibab Plateau. This one mile unveils 250 million years of geologic history. Each step down from the rim represents 20,000 years of history. Three steps off the rim and you've passed the time humans were part of earth's formula.

The Bright Angel and Kaibab trails are the most popular and are maintained by the National Forest Service. Hike them or take a mule ride down.

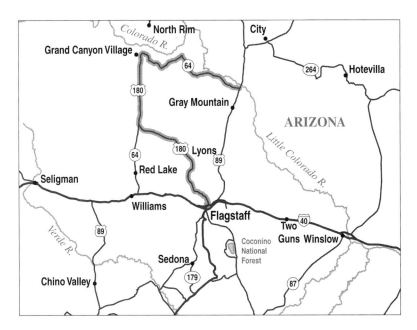

On the east rim drive near Desert View Campground is the less-used Tanner trail. Hike by clock, not by distance. For every hour down the canyon, plan on two hours up. I hiked to Plateau Point for a view of the Colorado River. It took just over two hours to reach the Plateau Point for a 360-degree view of agelessness, and four and a half to climb back to the rim. I earned my Grand Canyon Brew and Muleskinner Chili Beer with that hike. Fastest time, what the rangers call "Macho Time," for running 20 miles from the south rim to the north rim is three hours and nine minutes.

Staying on the rim, walk in the early morning and late afternoon for the best color. If you're lucky, you can watch a late afternoon thundershower travel the width of the canyon (did you just wish for rain?), sunlight refracted by the passing showers, the rain evaporating before it ever touches ground. The convoluted canyons, towering buttes, and silhouettes of shadowy bluffs will send shivers up your spine. These are Ansel Adams scenes for the amateur photographer.

Once out of the Grand Canyon National Park, the terrain opens up as Route 64 parallels the Little Colorado River.

Route 89 north completes the Grand Circle, or you can veer off at Route 264 into the "2 x Four Corners" section. If you take a straight shot south into Flagstaff, with the San Francisco Mountains and Humphreys Peak (at 12,643 feet) looming the whole way, your route intersects with roads in the "Hanging on the Mogollon Rim" section.

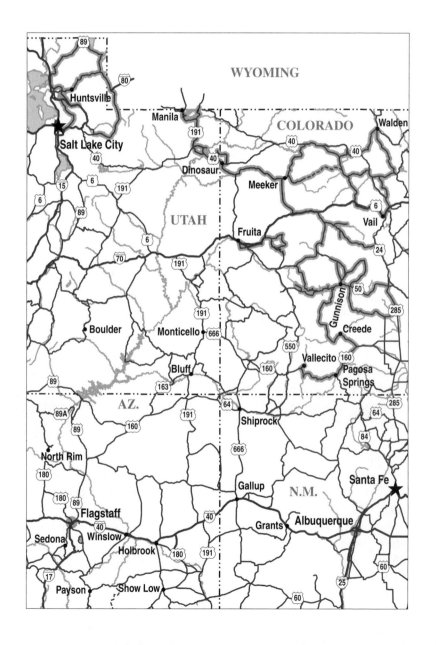

West Slope Slalom

"There is scarcely a more beautiful place on the face of the earth," wrote Captain J.N. Macomb, who led the first topographical survey of the western slope of Colorado. Here the air is cleaner, the population less, and the mountains more majestic. Practically every road is a scenic one. The asphalt is smoother, the rivers wilder, and even the roadbeds are pretty good.

The distances are greater, not just the surface plane but the vertical plane as well. From verdant valleys across vast wilderness areas to craggy peaks that inspire comparisons with European counterparts, the elevation varies from 4,000 feet above sea level to over 13,000 feet.

Beginning in the west with Utah's Rocky Mountain Province and covering the northwest quadrant of Colorado, these loops and trails travel heavily forested mountains, across 25 passes with names like Wolf, Gore, and Independence. Across the Colorado and Uncompahgre Plateaus, hug rivers traveling westward from the Continental Divide, in canyons named Black and valleys named Grand . . . .

Just you and the mountains. Adjustments in altitude cause changes in attitude.

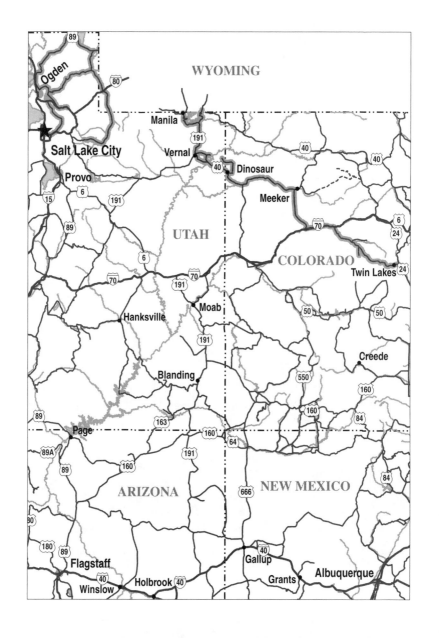

Rocky Mountain Province of Utah

The Basin and Range Province, in the western part of Utah, was named The Great Basin. In ancient times, this province was covered by Lake Bonneville, predecessor to the Great Salt Lake.

The Great Salt Lake is the largest lake west of the Mississippi, eight times saltier than the ocean and the second saltiest body of water on earth (the Dead Sea is numero uno). Since the lake has no outlet, the mineral salts that wash into it stay there—the lake is 27% salt.

Bordering the Great Basin to the northeast is the Rocky Mountain Province of Utah. The Wasatch and Uinta (oo-in-ta) mountain ranges reside here. Gnarled and steep, the Wasatch Range climbs over 11,000 feet. These are the mountains that surround **Salt Lake City**. The Uinta Range is the only major range in the "lower 48" that runs east-west. King's Peak, Utah's highest peak at 13,528 feet, is part of the range. Both of these ranges have vast National Forest land set aside.

The Shoshone tribe was located throughout northern Utah, southern Idaho, and western Wyoming long before the European invasion. Northern Utah was inhabited by the hunting and gathering bands of the Northwest Shoshones and some Utes. The Shoshones and Utes wandered from area to area on a network of well-established trails throughout the region. These trips do the same.

Home base is the National Forest Service's **Anderson Cove Campground** (801-745-3215) in **Huntsville**, Utah. Sitting directly on the Pineview Reservoir, you lose a little privacy with its developed sites, but gain a waterfront view. Loops B and C have campsites with a personal path to your own patch of sandy beach.

Trip 12 Salt Lake City Getaway Trail

Distance *70 miles*
Highlights *Over mountains, through canyons, across lakes to Grandmother's house*

THE ROUTE FROM SALT LAKE CITY

800 East turns into Emigration Canyon
Emigration Canyon to Route 65 north
Route 65 north to Route 66 north
Route 66 north to The Old Road west (it's the Frontage Road of I-84)
The Old Road west to Route 167 north
Route 167 north to Route 39 (home base choice for east or west)

The Shooting Star is the oldest saloon in Utah.

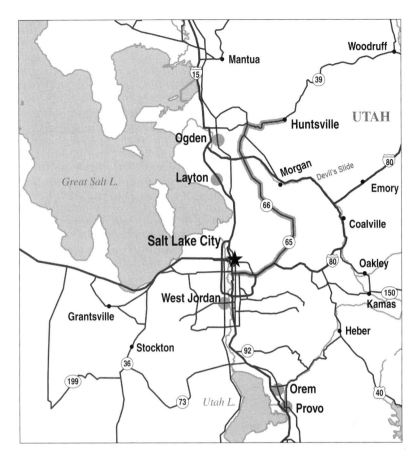

Given that **Salt Lake City** is a major departure point, the best way in and out is from the east. Bypassing the Interstate (one of my favorite things to do), take 800 east (in Salt Lake City the terms "street," "road," "boulevard," and "path" are not applied to their thoroughfares), which turns into Emigration Canyon. Part of the Pioneer Trail and the route of the infamous Donner Party (hungry for a manwich), this is a wild ride of curves and switchbacks to the top and over Big Mountain Summit and down to Route 65 north.

More red canyon curves meld with blue water at the East Canyon Reservoir, a busy water recreation area with boating and plenty of those water scooters. A hard left onto Route 66 north gets to S-turns so tight, 30 mph seems a challenge. Paralleling the East Canyon Creek, this sweet ride is why we motorcyclists have a passion for the sport. At Morgan go under the Interstate 84 overpass and take The Old Road to Mountain Green.

➡ ABBEY ROAD

Just getting lost looking for the good roads, I came across this little town oddity. On Route 39 in Huntsville is a sign pointing to Monastery. Thinking, "That's an odd but saintly name for a town," I followed the signs to . . . The Abbey of the Holy Trinity (www.holytrinityabbey.org, 801-745-3784). Ordain-airily, staying away from religion and politics is a good move, but the Trappist-Cistercian Monks bake delicious whole-wheat and raisin breads daily. The fruit, nut, or spice flavored creamed honey will curl your toes and spread the bread. After filling the snack sack and stomach, move to the chapel. It's open to everyone, and seven times a day the monks gather for Gregorian Chants. Visitors are welcome to attend. ■

At the Abbey of the Holy Trinity you'll find fresh bread and superb honey of several heavenly flavors.

The supermarket in **Morgan** is the last place for food on the way to the **Huntsville** home base without making a special trip. If you're choosing to set up camp first, though, the ride through Ogden Canyon to **Ogden** for food is a special trip to enjoy.

The Old Road connects with Route 167, a Utah Scenic Backway through the **Wasatch National Forest,** and leads right to Pineview Reservoir in the **Cache National Forest.** Go left, on Route 39 east, for **Anderson Cove Campground.**

Huntsville is a small, old town in Utah. In fact, the **Shooting Star Saloon** (801-745-2002) is the oldest bar in Utah. I asked the bartender, "how did a bar, in Utah, happen to be on the same block as a church and a school?" She replied, "It seems the pioneers planted first and built the Shooting Star second. Everything else came last."

Walking into the place immediately immerses you in western eclectic funk. Taking in the large mounted heads of the normal antlers and bared teeth variety, I did a double take. There in the center of the long wall was the largest Saint Bernard head I'd ever seen. Not your usual mounted head. The Saint Bernard is the mascot of the Shooting Star. It turns out the dog was the pet in residence at a similar western motif bar near Yellowstone National Park. When the dog died, the owner headed for the taxidermist. When he closed the bar, the head headed south for the winter and a new career at the Shooting Star Saloon.

Speaking about stuffed dogs, the Shooting Star Burger is a world famous meal consisting of two cheeseburgers topped with a Polish sausage, sauteed onions, and any other garnish.

The closest supermarket for fresh foods, from home base, is Ogden. The bonus, Route 39 west (a.k.a. Ogden Canyon Road) is eight miles of twisties with waterfalls and the Ogden River to make the chore a pleasure. Smith's supermarket is on the left as you enter civilization. Tie dinner down tight for the return ride or try **The Oaks** (www.xmission.com/~sambell/index.html, 801-394-2421). Situated on the river with both an outdoor patio and indoor dining, it offers a casual atmosphere for breakfast, hamburgers, and sandwiches.

Trip 13   Logan Canyon-Raspberry Fruit Loop

Distance *225 miles*

Highlights *Canyons, passes, fruit stands, raspberry heaven, lakes, and mountains. Did I mention curves and climbs?*

THE ROUTE FROM ANDERSON COVE CAMPGROUND, HUNTSVILLE

Route 39 west to Route 158 north (old Route 162)

Route 158 north to 5500 east

5500 east to 4200 north (left at T)

4200 north turns into 3100 north over the North Ogden Divide

3100 north to 500 west (left at the high school)

Waterfront sites make for quite the sights at Anderson Cove Campground, Huntsville, Utah.

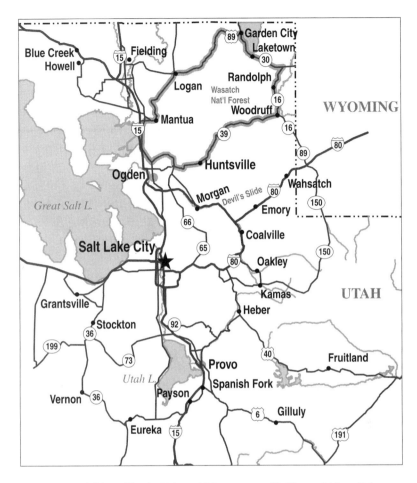

500 west to right on Elberta Drive which merges with Pleasant View Drive

Pleasantview Drive to right on 1000 west (signs for I-15 and Route 89)

1000 west to Route 89 north

Route 89 north to Route 30 east

Route 30 east to Route 16 south

Route 16 south to Route 39 west

Rounding the Pineview Reservoir, the road hugs cliff walls and the water. Just after the small town of **Eden** (yes, there are a couple of gardens), the climb over North Ogden Divide begins. Stop at the summit for vistas of the reservoir and valley to the east, Ogden and Salt Lake to the west. The descent into **Ogden** is another cliff-hanger.

If you're in Garden City in August, you can enjoy the annual raspberry festival, where all things raspberry are available to tempt your taste buds. It's on Route 89 at Bear Lake.

The only redeeming social value to Route 89 is the dozens of fruit stands in the apricot orchards on both sides of the road. The fruit stands offer the best in locally harvested fruits and veggies. Pick up a picnic for later.

Because of Logan's strategic location, it grew rapidly after its founding in 1859. The Shoshone called the area "the house of the Great Spirit." Early maps called it Willow Valley and the mouth of the canyon was called Logan's Hole after Ephraim Logan, a trapper. Logan River flows from the canyon but at one time was a tributary to the mighty Lake Bonneville, which was 650 feet above Logan's Main Street millions of years ago.

Logan Canyon is 40 miles of S-turns through the **Wasatch-Cache National Forest.** A popular route to Bear Lake, the road winds past lush green fields with plenty of passing opportunities. The slow climb from 4,700 feet to 7,800 feet continues through nearly vertical limestone canyon walls, giving way to mountain meadows, past Beaver Mountain and its summit. This leads to a stunning, sweeping view of turquoise-colored Bear Lake. On the way down to the lake, billboards start to dot the landscape, proclaiming raspberries in every shape, shake, and form. An annual August raspberry festival is held in **Garden City**, which is at the foot of Route 89 and Bear Lake. Raspberry Heaven shakes, ice cream, yogurt, and every other imaginable concoction to scarf the little suckers is blended on the shoreline of Bear Lake.

Here are the bare facts about Bear Lake. It sits at an elevation of 5,918 feet, is 20 miles long, eight miles wide, 208 feet deep, and has 48 miles of shoreline.

Route 30 parallels the shoreline, climbs out of the valley, then flattens out for 30 miles to **Woodruff**. Traveling west on Route 39 feels like an entirely different road from the Wasatch National Forest eastbound loop.

Trip 14   Wasatch National Forest Loop

Distance *210 miles*
Highlights *Switchbacks through pristine forest covering 12,000-foot mountain peaks, down valley roads with snow-capped panoramas, and up main streets of small-town Americana*

THE ROUTE FROM ANDERSON COVE CAMPGROUND, HUNTSVILLE

Utah Route 39 east to Route 16 south

Route 16 south turns into Wyoming Route 89 south

Route 89 south to Route 150 south

Route 150 south turns into Utah 150 south

Route 150 south to Route 32 north (signs to Wanship)

Route 32 north to The Old Road (bear left at the Spring Chicken Inn)

Wasatch National Forest is vast and largely a ride of solitude.

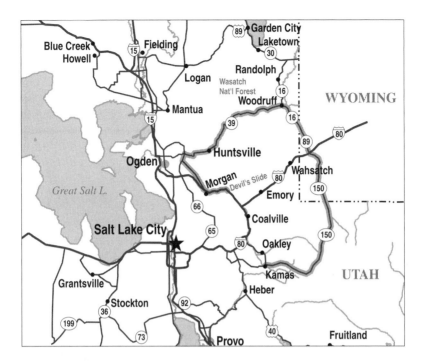

The Old Road turns into many Main Streets in many towns

The Old Road eventually turns into Route 86 west

Route 86 west to Interstate 84 west (sorry, but it's the only road past Devil's Slide)

Exit Interstate 84 at Morgan and go straight onto The Old Road

The Old Road to Route 167 north

Route 167 north to Route 39 and home base

You enter and exit the **Wasatch National Forest** three times on this loop. Starting strong from Pineview Reservoir, Route 39 climbs beside the South Fork of the Ogden River to high mountain meadow. A wide curvy road takes you from 6,000 feet to an August-snow-patched 8,500 feet. With panoramic views, places to picnic, and no one else around, these 50 miles are a perfect way to begin a day in the saddle. Be careful of cattle, which have free reign on the back side of the forest into **Woodruff.**

Woodruff is a one-convenience-store-gas-station junction. It's 30 miles to the next filling station in **Evanston,** Wyoming. This stretch of two-laner is a straight high plains ride with expansive views of snow-capped mountains to the northeast.

Devil's Slide looks more like a petrified prehistoric dinosaur than a geologic formation.

Exiting Wyoming means entering the Wasatch National Forest and straddling the border of the High Uintas Wilderness Area. Here ascend, via switchbacks and S-turns, some of the tallest peaks around. Haden Peak, at 12,479 feet, and Mount Agassiz, at 12,428 feet, both rising above treeline with August snowcaps, are viewed from a distance and up close throughout this section of asphalt. There are plenty of viewpoints and picnic areas beside lakes named Mirror and Pass. The backside of Route 150 follows the flow of the Upper Provo River past Provo Falls and State Gorge. Both have turnouts.

Route 150 dumps you into **Kamas** and Route 32 north. There are signs, but from here it's names of towns instead of route numbers. There is one tricky section when you leave Route 32 behind. At the Spring Chicken Inn (no comment), Route 32 bears right under Interstate 80. Where Route 32 bears right, take the Old Road, by staying straight. This is a frontage road which parallels Interstate 80, adding curves and subtracting eighteen-wheelers. Eventually merging with Interstate 80, you'll ride past Devil Slide. There is a scenic turnout across from this geologic oddity that looks like the back of a giant stegosaur. Jump off Interstate 80 to the Old Road at **Morgan,** only eight miles up from Devil Slide.

The Old Road connects with Route 167, a Utah Scenic Backway, and enters Wasatch National Forest for a third time this loop. The scenic backway is literally a back way into Pineview Reservoir and Route 39 for home base.

Trip 15   Flaming Gorge to Dinosaur Nat'l Monument Trail

Distance *215 miles*

Highlights *Mountains, gorgeous gorge, switchbacks, and time travel to when the earth was young and humans but a gleam in Mother Nature's eye. Whether you're a child or with one, this is a history and geology education come alive.*

THE ROUTE FROM MANILA, UTAH

Route 44 south to Route 191 north

Return Route 191 south to Route 40 east

Route 40 east to Route 149 north

Route 149 north to Dinosaur National Monument Visitor Center

Route 149 south to Route 40 east

Route 40 east to Harpers Corner Drive (Colorado entrance to Dinosaur National Monument)

Return Harpers Corner Drive to Route 40

The lookout over Flaming Gorge National Recreation Area takes your breath away.

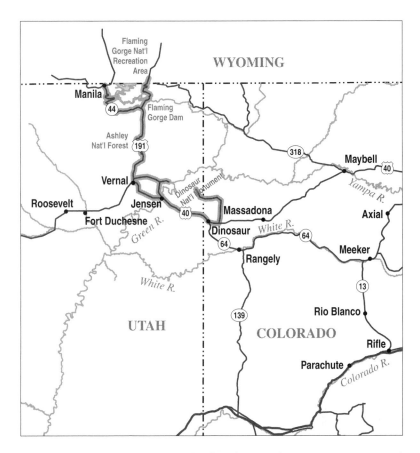

Although I call this a trail, spend a few days at **Flaming Gorge National Recreation Area** (www.utah.com/nationalsites/flaming_gorge.htm, 435-784-3445). Within the **Ashley National Forest,** Flaming Gorge is a wonderful exploration of geological history, pioneer efforts, and big game animals. If you fish, this is Mecca with routine trophy catches. A recent record Mackinaw trout weighed 51 pounds!

A tour of the **Flaming Gorge Dam,** 502 feet above the bedrock, not only provides an in-depth look at hydro-electric production, but also shows how management of water levels contributes to record catches. Constant lake temperatures in the mid-fifties Fahrenheit are ideal for nurturing the food chain that creates year-round trophy fishing. There are many campgrounds along the 91-mile-long reservoir, ranging from remote to developed. Convenient **Cedar Springs,** with a water view in sites #5 through #8, is close to the dam.

FINDING THE WORDS TO DESCRIBE FLAMING GORGE

Major John Wesley Powell, the first person to record his exploration of the entire Colorado River, wrote on June 2, 1869, "At a distance of one to 20 miles, a brilliant red gorge is seen, the red being surrounded by broad bands of mottled buff and gray at the summit of the cliffs, and curving down to the water's edge on the nearer slope of the mountain. This is where the river enters the mountain range—the head of the first canyon we are to explore, or rather, an introductory canyon to a series made by the river through the range. We have named it Flaming Gorge." ■

At the U.S. Forest Ranger Station in **Manila,** buy a "Wheels of Time" self-guided tour. It takes you through the Sheep Creek Canyon Loop Road, a narrow and steep path to 600-million-year old rock, some of the most ancient geology in North America. The dramatic uplifted north flank of the Uinta Mountains, with great thrust faults and colorful landscape, exposes the different layers of its formation like a cleaved onion. The Sheep Creek Canyon Loop Road starts seven miles south of Manila.

Sheep Creek Canyon travels through the "Wheels of Time." Try 600 million years of geology.

> **➡ REMOTE ACCESS**
>
> Twenty-one miles up Harpers Corner Scenic Drive is Echo Park Road. The confluence of the Green and Yampa Rivers at Echo Park has created Sand Canyon, a scenic cleft in the gorgeous, cream-colored Weber sandstone. It is one of the most beautiful spots on the continent. The ancient Fremont people must have thought so too, for they left a message rock covered with petroglyphs to record their travels through this spot a thousand years ago. The Yampa River is the last wild (not dammed or is that damned?) river in Colorado.
>
> Echo Park Road, like the Yampa River, is untamed as well. This is a steep 13 miles of challenging, sandy, switchbacked desert road. The road descends through the red beds of Moenkopi Formation, and then drops into Sand Canyon. They didn't name it Sand Canyon without reason—if it rains the road is impassable. Echo Park campground, with only nine sites, is nestled at the confluence of the Green and Yampa. There is plenty of room if the sites are filled, although they rarely are. Water and pit toilets are provided in the summer. This ride is for the hardy (or foolhardy) but worth it.   ■

If you're lucky, when you pass the first cattle guard, you'll see a herd of bighorn sheep grazing. Slow down and keep a low rev, because if you scare the alpha ewe, they'll bolt.

It's worth backtracking the section of Route 44 circumvented by Sheep Creek Canyon Loop Road for million-dollar views of Sheep Creek Bay and Flaming Gorge.

At Flaming Gorge's Red Canyon visitor center an easy trail along the rim, 1,360 feet above the water, is a mandatory look-see. Heading for the dam, take a side trip to Swett Ranch for a view into family ranching, pioneering life, and perseverance. The short dirt road to the historical site is no swett (pun intended). Past the dam, take a quick right and descend to the spillway, where various amphibious craft are launched and trophy fish caught.

Back on Route 191 north, head out to Antelope Flats to see a herd of the fastest animals in North America leap and bound. Turn around and head for **Vernal** and **Dinosaur National Monument** (www.nps.gov/dino, 970-374-3000). From Flaming Gorge to Vernal is a 10-switchback descent (darn)!

The visitor center at Dinosaur National Monument is built into a quarry of dinosaur bones.

Twenty miles east of Vernal is Dinosaur National Monument, a legacy of rivers past and present. Preserved in the sandbar of an ancient river is a time capsule from the world of dinosaurs. The Utah side of the national monument, seven miles north of Jensen, contains a visitor center, where a quarry

Echo Park Road offers some of the most spectacular views on this continent, however its 13 miles of steep, sandy switchbacks will test your dual-sport riding ability.

Echo Park is at the confluence of the Yampa and Green Rivers. It is the beginning of the Grand River, which is now the Colorado River.

wall containing the world's largest discovery of Jurassic period dinosaur bones is incorporated into the building. Built to protect over 2,000 bones, the visitor center allows you to see and touch actual fossilized bones and reconstructed dinosaurs.

The visitor center on the Colorado side of the monument, two miles past the town of Dinosaur, is the gateway to canyon country carved by the rivers of the present. The Harpers Corner Scenic Drive takes about two hours, even though the round trip is only 50 miles. From roadside turnouts, scan the rugged landscape formed by the Green and Yampa Rivers. This confluence creates the Colorado River. In earlier times the Colorado River was named the Grand River . . . hence Grand Junction, Grand Canyon, etc.

Trip 16   Flowing Along the Rivers Trail

Distance   *296 miles*
Highlights   *Long sweepers with flowing water, a 12,000-foot pass, and big-bucks ski towns. A two-day trail if spending time visiting the towns and villages, soaking in hot springs, or anything else besides riding*

THE ROUTE FROM DINOSAUR NATIONAL MONUMENT

Route 64 east to Route 13 South

Route 13 south to Route 6 east

Route 6 east to Interstate 70 east (sorry, but it's only seven miles)

Interstate 70 east to Route 82 east

Route 82 east to Snowmass Village and return to Route 82 east

Route 82 east ends at Route 24 junction

Return 82 west to Basalt turnoff

Through Basalt Center to Frying Pan Road

On the way to home base, you'll have a magnificent view of the Ruedi Reservoir.

The landscape of Rio Blanco County, a place early Ute called "the land of shining mountains," is a study in contrast. The White River cuts across the high desert plateau from **Rangely** to the pastoral valleys of Meeker. **Meeker** to **Rifle** follows Sheep Creek. Rifle and **Rifle Creek** got their names from a mapmaker in the 1876 Hayden Survey expedition. Seems he had to draw directions on a map so someone could return to the site where he left his rifle.

Rifle to **Glenwood Springs** follows the Colorado River. Glenwood Springs, nestled below the escarpment of Red Mountain, is home to the famous **Hot Springs Pool.** The world's largest outdoor thermal pool packs them in year-round. **Doc Holliday's Grave** is a 15-minute walk above the town to Linwood Cemetery.

The **Hotel Colorado** (www.hotelcolorado.com, 800-544-3998) was originally part of the Hot Springs and Vapor Caves Complex. Built in 1893, it was the western summer White House for President Theodore Roosevelt.

HOW TEDDY GOT HIS NAME

Seems President Roosevelt hunted in the White River National Forest when visiting the area. His favorite hunting target was bear. One day in 1905, he returned from a hunt empty-handed. The maids at the hotel, feeling sorry for the President, made him a bear out of rags and gave it to Teddy. Because of this gesture, we see all those Teddy Bears on the back of everybody's bike. If you need a Teddy Bear for those insecure days, Teddy's Corner at the Hotel Colorado specializes in the little, furry, consoling animals. ∎

A side trip through Glenwood Canyon on Interstate 70 toward **Eagle** is a 15-minute drive through 1,800-foot-high walls adjacent to the Colorado River. A chance to break your neck looking up instead of down in Colorado. A 1.2-mile hike to Hanging Lake is a definite if you want to dismount.

Picking up the rivers again, follow the Roaring Fork River from Glenwood Springs to Basalt, then follow the Frying Pan River from **Basalt** to home base, the **Ruedi** (roo-dye) **Reservoir Campground** (970-963-2266) at **Ruedi Dam.**

You can produce some high-flame exhaust following the Frying Pan River. It's another 15 miles along the red rock edge of the reservoir on a real cliff-hanger of a road with lots of twisties to an even more remote National Forest Service Campground. You'll climb higher than Aspen following Frying Pan Road to the end of the asphalt. This road offers spectacular views of the reservoir and the Continental Divide.

Following Route 82 southeast of Basalt brings you to the big bucks country of **Snowmass** and **Aspen.**

Take Brush Creek Road (sign says Snowmass Village) to the top. Bear right at the fork (Campground/Divide Parking Road) and park in the lot for **Krabloonik Restaurant and Kennel** (www.krabloonik.com, 970-923-3953). Krabloonik means "big eyebrows" an Inuit term for "white man." The restaurant is open for dinner and specializes in wild game. Elk, caribou, quail, pheasant, boar, and various fish are offered on a menu that changes weekly. Specialties of the non-game variety include wild mushroom soup and fresh-baked breads with homemade preserves. View Mt. Daly and Capitol Peak for Sunday Brunch.

The largest sled dog kennel in North America offers tours of the kennel, home to owner/operator MacEachen's sled dogs. Dan competed in the

"Last Great Race," the Iditarod, a 1,049-mile race from Anchorage to Nome, Alaska. The educational kennel tour, Tuesday through Sunday at 11:00 a.m. and 2:30 p.m., provides insight into sled dog racing and breeding. The dogs are hybrids of three original sled dog types: Malamute, Eskimo, and Siberian, commonly referred to as a Husky.

Aspen, an old mining town turned ski and summer resort, is where the billionaires are pushing the millionaires to **Vail**. The village is worth stopping in to gawk at the rich and famous strolling about. As a friend of mine once said, "It's the Gucci-est of places."

Aspen's most redeeming feature is its proximity to Independence Pass. At 12,096 feet, you get a great snaking climb to the summit and crossing of the Continental Divide. Four miles before this top-of-the-world view is the ghost town of Independence.

Thirteen and a half miles outside of Aspen, the Independence Lode was discovered on July 4, 1879. It had to be summer—at 10,900 feet, you could hardly break ground given a snow cover from early October to late May. The town of **Independence**, the first community in the Roaring Fork Valley, lasted ten years, competing with another town founded the same year, Aspen. Easy to see who survived, but the buildings of Independence still intrigue the wanderer.

From here, connect with the "Front Range" section via Route 24 instead of returning on Route 82 west. Move to a new home base at **Curecanti National Recreation Area** via Trip 17.

The author takes time for a photo-op with some new friends atop Independence Pass.

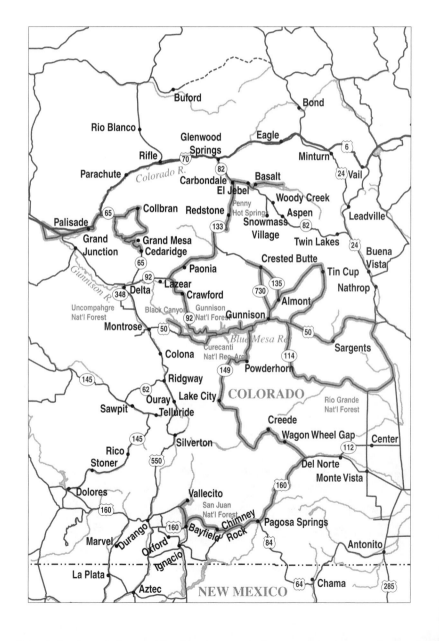

Gunnison National Forest

Home base for these next three trips, and a link to the "2 x Four Corners" section, is **Curecanti National Recreation Area** (www.nps.gov/cure, 970-641-2337) There are many campgrounds in Curecanti to meet your specific desires, but **Dry Gulch Campground** is a less well known and therefore less populated (nine sites) environment. Although water and pit toilets are standard, the Elk Creek Visitor Center/Marina/Restaurant/Showers (bring quarters), on Blue Mesa Lake, is only a mile and a half away. Blue Mesa Lake, 20 miles long with 96 miles of shoreline, is the largest man-made lake in Colorado.

The human history of Curecanti and the surrounding area dates back to at least 8,000 B.C. Archeologists have uncovered remains of wickiups, commonly known as tipis, 4,500 years old. Utes summered here and wintered in nearby Montrose. Fur traders and miners explored the region as the northern branch of the Spanish Trail from Santa Fe to Los Angeles. Captain John Gunnison and his survey party explored the area in 1854. A narrow gauge railroad, the **Denver & Rio Grande Railroad Western,** bearing the Curecanti Needle as its logo, operated from 1882 to 1949. I arrived in Cimarron on August 13th, the anniversary date of its first arrival into Cimarron. We'll ride its old railroad bed over Marshall Pass on Trip 18.

You won't find traffic jams in downtown Tincup, Colorado.

Trip 17 West Elk Trail

Distance *258 miles*

Highlights *Curves and ever-tightening curves, from valley roads hanging next to rivers to mountain meadows at 10,000 feet. Challenges range from 15 mph cliff-hangers to 55 mph S-turns, while sneaking a peek at the peaks.*

THE ROUTE FROM RUEDI DAM

Frying Pan River Road to Route 82 west

Route 82 west to Route 133 south

Route 133 south to Route 92 east

Route 92 east to Route 50 east. *

Route 50 east to Route 135 north

Route 135 north to left on White Rock Road (it's across from the Crested Butte Center for the Arts). Follow signs to Kebler Pass

Turn around at Kebler Pass and take first right (signs to Ohio Pass). It is Gunnison County 730 south (no markings)

Gunnison County 730 to Route 135 south

Route 135 south to Route 50 west

The elegant Clevehorn Manor may stretch your budget but your stay there will be a memorable one.

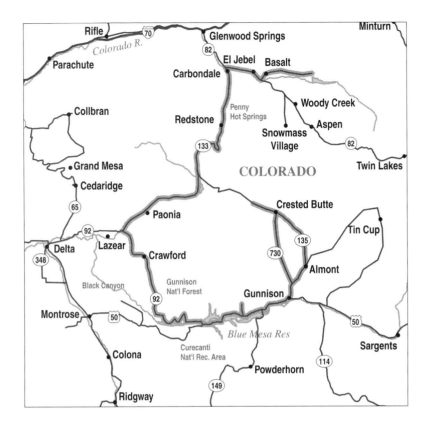

* ALTERNATE ROUTE

If loaded, set up home base at Dry Gulch before tackling the good gravel
road passes. If stopping along the way for a natural hot springs soak or
side trips, allow yourself two days.

Outside of **Carbondale**, the first enjoyable stop is **Penny Hot Springs,** a
natural spring bubbling beside the Crystal River. To find it, go 0.8 miles
past the 56-mile marker, 0.2 miles past the 55-mile marker going north.
The road widens at this point and on the northbound side of Route 133 is a
small gravel turnout. Park, go down a 30-foot embankment, and you'll see
the one- and two-person pools created by rock piles. Using rocks, adjust the
temperature of the pool by controlling the amount of river water flowing
into it. It's too hot straight out of the earth.

The gingerbread village of **Redstone**, self-proclaimed "Ruby of the
Rockies," is nestled deep in the Elk Mountains. Take the north entrance to
Redstone (sign) off Route 133. Be careful, the road has these bottoming-out
dips for drainage through the town. Pay heed to the signs!

Your bath is already drawn at Penny Hot Springs.

Just before you complete the loop through town you'll see a dirt parking lot on your left. The road leads to the **Clevehorn Manor,** a castle built by John Cleveland Osgood, financier, coal baron, and founder-director of the Colorado Fuel and Iron Company. Clevehorn Manor was finished in 1903 for Osgood and his second wife, Alma Regina Shelgram, a Swedish woman 20 years his junior who was known as "Lady Bountiful." The original estate included the 42-room manor house, a 40-room inn, 84 cottages, 4,200 acres of scenic land, and a railroad.

The **Redstone Inn** (www.redstoneinn.com, 800-748-2524), built as a complete hotel for Osgood's miners and their guests, replicates a Dutch tavern, with a tall clock tower and cut-stone fireplace incorporated into the design. The inn offers all the modern conveniences.

The giant beehives across the road from your return to Route 133 south, are coke ovens built by Osgood for his coal mining operations. The coal was loaded from the top and heated to a very high temperature to eliminate all volatile materials.

The trail continues up and over McClure Pass, at 8,755 feet, past Paonia Reservoir, picking up the Gunnison River and a scenic shot into **Paonia**. Paonia is best known for its orchards and veggies. Samuel Wade, the town's founder, named the town for the peony plant roots he brought to the valley.

Paonia is also the meeting spot for bike rallies throughout the summer. It's a hospitable town with live music being performed somewhere most nights. In fact, this little valley offers a lot of Bluegrass music. The town of **Crawford** even has its own recording studio.

After Crawford the fun turns to challenge and danger. Up to now, the West Elk Trail has been like S-ing the silhouetted edge of an elk's rack. Beginning at **Gunnison National Forest**, in full view of the majestic Ragged Mountains, the road becomes hot, as dangerous as it is beautiful. Drop-offs of a thousand feet from the guardrail-less edge make an 11 out of a 10. Like the sirens of lore, these vistas beckon for a look, and of course your bike follows. Next thing you know you're across the white line, into the gravel, and adios.

Beehives for killer bees? No. These are the coke ovens at Redstone, built by John Osgood for his coal mining operations.

Another phenomenon to be aware of is the strange effect mud slides have on pavement in these parts. Here the mud flows under the road, heaving the asphalt up, so on some curves you lose traction when you're uplifted. With some driving sanity (and I know it's going to be tough), this road rivals any for the best in sustained curves and awesome scenery in the United States.

Gunnison, lying at the confluence of the Gunnison River and Tomichi Creek, is a western town in its feel and flavor. It is also the closest town for grocery shopping and other catch-up things.

Crested Butte is a funky old Victorian mining town. The entire town was designated a Historic Landmark District in 1974, and maintains a charm that Vail and Aspen never had. Good music and food can be had most everywhere. Outdoor cafes allow the steady flow of human entertainment to be appreciated. The expensive modern ski area Mt. Crested Butte is three miles above the town. Check out the **Mountain Bike Hall of Fame** (www.mtnbikehalloffame.com, 970-349-6817).

Kebler Pass Road starts out paved but quickly turns to good gravel roadbed. From Crested Butte, at 9,000 feet, it's a gradual wind through America's largest aspen stand and the massive Elk Mountains to **Kebler** at 9,980 feet. At the top of the pass the road narrows to a one-lane, two-rut,

On the Kebler Pass road you may have to share the right-of-way with other steeds. Note the classy trailer.

Great views are abundant on the road to beautiful Ohio Pass.

fifty-yard opening. Vistas everywhere. There's even a gravestone marking the now non-existent town of Irwin. At the summit you have a choice to make: Follow the loop directions, or continue on to Route 133 above Paonia and take the Gunnison National Forest cliff ride again.

Turning around and going over Ohio Pass, at 10,033 feet, brings you to a wide, mountain summit meadow to frolic in. Wildflowers are everywhere with reds, yellows, blues, and magentas galore. It's like crashing into Oz from Kansas. Descending from Ohio Pass, the road narrows, stays firm and is lined with tall aspens glittering in the sun and breeze. Pass by the Castles, spires carved from the West Elk volcano. This county road winds down to Route 135, five miles above Gunnison, and is one of the finer gravel roads to ride on. But, as with any challenge, check the local conditions before you go. If the sky looks threatening, reverse the route and climb Ohio Pass to Kebler Pass, then descend into Crested Butte. That way the asphalt home comes later in the day.

If you choose to stay on Route 133, you'll add three more hours to your ride. Crossing Kebler Pass, the gravel thickens and is a little more treacherous. Don't get caught in those late afternoon Colorado thunderstorms or the road will quickly turn to icemud.

Trip 18 Ghost Towns and Railroad Beds

Distance *235 miles*
Highlights *Four passes, two remote solid railroad bed passes and two highway passes that you wouldn't recognize without the signs. Mostly a scenic ride with about 50 miles of tight canyon twisties and hairpin climbs. Plenty of mining history and large game sightings probable*

THE ROUTE FROM CURECANTI NATIONAL RECREATION AREA

Route 50 east to Route 135 north
Route 135 north to National Forest Service 742 (signs to Tincup)
NFS 742 north to Gunnison County 765 south
Gunnison County 765 south to Gunnison County 76 south
Gunnison County 76 south to Route 50 east
Route 50 east to Marshall Pass Road (sign after gas station/bar/restaurant)
Marshall Pass Road to Route 285 south
Route 285 south to Route 114 west
Route 114 west to Route 50 east

The ride to **Gunnison** from home base hugs cliffs on the left and the shoreline of Blue Mesa Lake on the right. Two out of three days there is a speed trap between the lake and Gunnison, so relax and enjoy the scenery. Gunnison, an important railhead during the mining era, still has the friendly spirit of the old west.

When you branch off Route 135 at **Almont** for **Tincup**, the road narrows and climbs beside Taylor River through Taylor Canyon. This beautiful ride provides lots of curves, plenty of primitive camping, and granite rock walls sheer enough to attract many climbers. There are a number of places to stop and catch climbers doing their thing.

At **Taylor Park**, bear right onto County 765. The asphalt gives way to flat, solid roadbed good enough for me to pass a couple of dirt bikers. A gentle climb approaches Tincup, a partially restored mining town. It's like slipping back to an earlier era.

Check out Mirror Lake, a left just after town, or head straight for Cumberland Pass, an even 12,000 feet above sea level. Way above tree-line, passing many abandoned one-room cabins, Cumberland Pass offers a top-of-the-world view. Down the other side to **Pitkin**, it's about 22 miles of gravel.

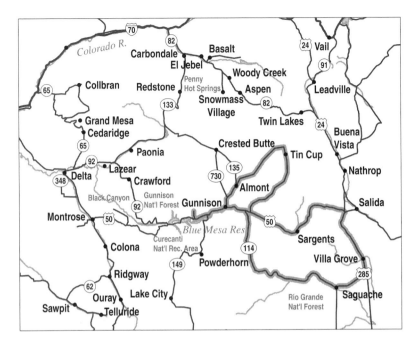

Pitkin, named for Frederick W. Pitkin, the second governor of Colorado, is a mining ghost town brought back from the dead. The town offers a museum, general store, rustic hotel, and asphalt. The next mining town, **Ohio City,** sitting along Quartz Creek, was established in 1879 as a gold and silver camp. Many old wooden structures survived and so do a few year-round residents.

Back on Route 50 east it's a short 20 miles to **Sargents** and the old **Denver & Rio Grand Western Railroad** bed across Marshall Pass. This 25 miles of roadbed winds its way over the Continental Divide. One time I passed through after a rain and a herd of bighorn sheep were surrounding a natural salt lick like bees to honey. I watched them resting on their knees, enjoying their treat, for ten minutes until the alpha ewe bolted.

Just after hitting the pavement again, head south, cross Poncha Pass, at 9,010 feet. Then it's a Bonneville Salt Flat straightaway to **Saguache** (Sa-Watch). You can really air it out on this stretch of road, occasionally peeking at the peaks of the San Luis Mountains.

Route 114 starts out with broad sweepers on high range country, and crosses the Continental Divide at North Pass (10,149 feet). The road from North Pass to Route 50 then smooths and narrows. The asphalt is banked perfectly as it descends into canyon curves, coming fast and tight. It's a great road to finish on with an easy ride home.

Trip 19   Black Canyon and Black Coal Railroads Loop

Distance   *100 miles*

Highlights   *Railroad history and two billion years of erosion. You can add miles if you stay on your bike rather than explore on foot.*

The Black Canyon of the Gunnison National Monument owes its name to the shadows created by its depth and steep walls.

THE ROUTE FROM CURECANTI NATIONAL RECREATION AREA

Route 50 west to Route 347 north
Route 347 north to end and return
Route 347 south to Route 50 east

This loop is short on miles but long on sightseeing. Following the Gunnison River, on the south side of the Blue Mesa Reservoir, is an immediate descent. You can feel the temperature rise as the road drops over the 17 miles to Cimarron.

Cimarron, within the **Curecanti National Recreation Area,** houses a remarkable exhibit of narrow gauge railroad history.

The narrow gauge exhibit contains two 1904 vintage stock cars, an 1883 outfit car, and a hand derrick crane car. Locomotive #278, built in 1882 and in service for 71 years, is a mile up the curvy canyon road heading for the 469 foot **Morrow Point Dam** (self-guided tour available, check at the visitor center).

Wolf Creek Pass is one of the many crossings you'll make of the Continental Divide.

The National Park Service also preserves a two-billion-year-old natural wonder, the **Black Canyon** of the **Gunnison National Monument** (www.nps.gov/blca, 970-641-2337), a marvel of nature's forces.

 NARROW GAUGE RAILROADS

The narrow gauge Denver & Rio Grande Western Railroad was the brain-child of William Jackson Palmer. The distance between rails was three feet, resulting in decreased costs for railbed, tunneling, rock cutting, and bridging—ideal for the remote coal and precious metal mining in the high Colorado mountains.

In January 1881, Palmer authorized a survey of the proposed route through the Black Canyon and began actual construction that spring. The first train steamed into Cimarron on August 13, 1882. The rails were removed in 1949 and the town disappeared, but the original trestle over Cimarron Creek remained and the National Park Service had the foresight to place a boxcar, caboose, coal tender, and old Locomotive #278 on the trestle. The National Park Service exhibit opened on the centennial of the first train to Cimarron. ∎

"Several western canyons exceed the Black Canyon in overall size," Wallace Hansen wrote after studying the geology of the region for a number of years. "Some are longer, some are deeper, some are narrower, and a few have walls as steep. But no other canyon in North America combines the depth, narrowness, sheerness, and somber countenance of the Black Canyon of the Gunnison."

The Black Canyon is 53 miles long. The 12-mile gorge is so steep (1,700 to 2,700 feet) that most of its walls are constantly shrouded in heavy shadows, thus its name. At one point the canyon is 1,300 feet wide at the top and 40 feet narrow at the bottom. Off-roaders, just after the entrance to the park take the road marked "East Portal" for a bottoms-up view of the gorge.

The Gunnison River within the Black Canyon drops an average of 95 feet per mile. This is one of the greatest rates of fall for a river in North America. There are 13 pullouts and hikes to the edge range from 300 feet to 3/4 of a mile. Bring some food and have a picnic by Sunset Point, High Point, Painted Wall, or my favorite, Dragon Point. If you want more miles, go west to **Montrose,** north to **Delta,** then east to **Hotchkiss** and back on the Gunnison National Forest Cliff Drive.

Trip 20 Silver Thread Trail

Distance *229 miles*

Highlights *Three passes from home base in Curecanti National Recreation Area to home base at Lemon Dam above Bayfield, northeast of Durango. Lots of history, scenery, and a few tight curves through canyons and over mountains and the Continental Divide*

THE ROUTE FROM CURECANTI NATIONAL RECREATION AREA

Route 50 west to Route 149 south

Route 149 south to Route 160 west

Route 160 west to La Plata County Route 501 (follow signs to Vallecito Lake)

La Plata County 501 to La Plata County 240 (follow signs to Lemon Dam)

La Plata County 240 to La Plata County 243 (Millers Creek Campground)

It's hard to say good-bye to Curecanti but more adventure lies ahead, with tales of food ranging from miners' stew to a stew of miners.

Here's a view of the San Juan Mountains and the headwaters of the Rio Grande River. This water eventually wends its way 1,850 miles downstream to the Gulf of Mexico.

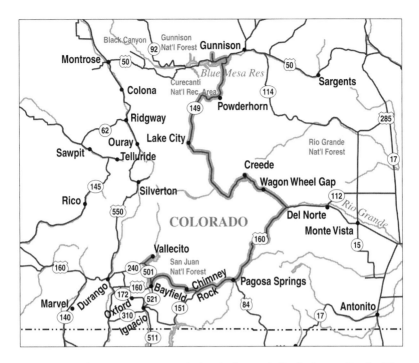

Leaving Blue Mesa Reservoir behind, the road climbs immediately. The Silver Thread Trail, though once a toll road and stage route for miners, smoothly weaves through the **Gunnison** and **Rio Grande National Forests.** Riding the high plains, the road slowly narrows as it enters the valley following the Lake Fork of the Gunnison River. It feels like steep canyon walls are rising as you enter the San Juan Mountains, often called the "Little Switzerland of the Rockies," and Lake City.

Lake City is the largest Historic District in Colorado and the highest county in the "lower 48." At 8,670 feet, the area was bypassed for early settlement. When Enos Hotchkiss's discovery of a rich lode in 1874 became known, that quickly changed. Originally named the Golden Fleece, the mine remained a producer for more than 50 years.

Lake City's best known historical figure is **Alferd Packer.** Alferd was hired to guide a party of five men to the gold fields. They got lost in the rugged San Juans in the middle of the winter. Next spring, Alferd showed up at a nearby Indian Agency without his party but with some strange looking beef jerky in his saddlebags. Ultimately admitting to partaking of his brethren, but denying murder, he was convicted of manslaughter and sentenced to 40 years. The Alferd Packer massacre site is four miles south of Lake City, past Lake San Cristobal, at the base of the (Hannibal the) Cannibal Plateau.

Lake San Cristobal, the second largest natural lake in Colorado, was created by the Slumgullion Slide. The 700-year-old mud flow is four miles long and 2,000 feet wide. Some sections are moving 28 feet a year. Decades ago, the earth flow dammed the Lake Fork of the Gunnison River and created the three-square mile lake.

The steep ascent of 11,361-foot Slumgullion Pass crosses the earth flow. The name comes from the resemblance the yellowish mud has to a thick miners' stew, Slumgullion Stew, made of everything in camp that could be eaten. Originally created by the Donner Party, it was modified by Alferd Packer.

Stop at the Windy Point Lookout for a panorama of the Black Canyon and the rugged San Juans 30 miles beyond. Then head for the Divide at 10,901-foot Spring Creek Pass. Going downhill to cross the Continental Divide is pretty bizarre.

Just after Spring Creek Pass is a scenic lookout on the right. A long look over the valley to the San Juan Mountains reveals the Rio Grande Pyramid. It is the headwaters of the Rio Grande River and its 1,850-mile journey to the Gulf of Mexico.

Creede, a historic silver mining town still clinging to its roots, sits at 8,800 feet.

There is no active mining now, but Creede has an underground mining museum, and a nationally acclaimed repertory theater. South of Creede is Wagon Wheel Gap. The hot spring at the gap was a favorite spot for the Utes and their famous leader, **Chief Ouray.** The bathhouse is now privately owned.

   A SILVER LINING

Nicholas Creede created a stampede when he discovered the mine he named by exclaiming "Holy Moses." "Don't jostle that fellow. He may become a millionaire tomorrow," became a town slogan.

By 1892, $1,000,000 worth of silver had been mined. A boomtown draws more than miners, and soon gamblers, saloon keepers, and prostitutes followed. Bat Masterson operated a saloon, Poker Alice won big, while the Mormon Queen, Lulu Slain, and Slanting Annie practiced their trade. An article in the *Creede Candle* said, "Creede is unfortunate in getting more of the flotsam of the state than usually falls to the lot of a mining camp. Some of her citizens would take a prize in a hog show." ■

A fellow rider puts on all-you-can-eat barbecues at Brown's Sandwich Shop.

The route continues through South Fork with its RV parks and motels. Just east of South Fork on Route 160 is **Brown's Sandwich Shop** (719-873-5582). Brown's puts together a great and inexpensive open-pit barbeque feed. All-you-can-eat barbequed brisket and ribs, homemade sauces and gravies, coupled with a buffet means racheting up those shocks a few notches when you're finished eating here.

Now that you've bulked up, start following the South Fork of the Rio Grande River up and over the Continental Divide via Wolf Creek Pass at 10,857 feet. Named for squatter-trapper **Bill Wolf,** the pass was completed in 1916.

Just before the pass is a three-mile dirt road called Lobo Lookout. A spectacular vantage point and picnic area sits on the topological crest of the mountain. Wolf Creek Ski Area has an average snowfall of 435 inches and is 10,600 feet at the base and 11,775 at the summit. Snow can fall here any time of year.

Slowly and with a three-laner descent, land in **Pagosa Springs.** Pagosa Springs took its name from the Ute, who called the hot springs "Pagosah," or "boiling waters." Most of the municipal buildings are heated with geothermal energy.

Take Route 160 to home base. If you are moving on, Trip 41 visits Chimney Rock Anasazi Ruins and other western and Native American Indian treasures. See "2 x Four Corners" section.

Trip 21 Grand Mesa Loop

Distance *150 miles*
Highlights *The spectacular Grand Mesa*

THE ROUTE FROM COLORADO NATIONAL MONUMENT

Left on Rim Rock Drive (to Grand Junction)
Rim Rock Drive to left on Monument Road
Monument Road to Route 340 east
Route 340 east to Route 6 east (follow signs)

Rim Rock Drive, in the Colorado National Monument is your driveway to homebase.

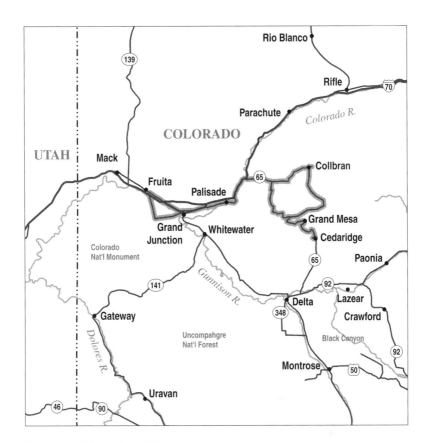

Route 6 east to Business 70 east

Business 70 east to Interstate 70 east. (sorry, but it's only three exits)

Interstate 70 east to Route 65 south

Route 65 south to Cedaredge, turn around

Route 65 north to right on National Forest Service 121 (sign to Alexander Lake)

NFS 121 to Route 330 west at Collbran

Route 330 west to Route 65 north

Route 65 north to Interstate 70 west

Interstate 70 west to Business 70 west

Business 70 west to Route 6 west (wait for 2nd sign before bearing right)

Route 6 west to Route 340 west

Route 340 west to Monument Road

Monument Road to Colorado National Monument entrance and Rim Rock Drive

Fruita, Colorado, is dinosaur country. Headquartered there is Dinamation International Society, the research arm of a company that makes animated creatures you see in the movies.

Home base for this loop is a little-known gem, **Colorado National Monument** (www.nps.gov/colm, 970-858-3617). Built on the edge of the Uncompahgre Plateau Uplift, campsites are on the edge (sites 47, 49, 51) of a sheer 1,500-foot cliff, overlooking the entire Grand Valley. The monument is sheer, red-walled canyons, sandstone formations, and colorful desert scenery carved by wind, water, and time. At night, a full moon bright enough to require sunglasses saves the lantern juice. Shooting stars, a view of Grand Mesa, and the opposing Colorado Plateau make this an extraordinary setting. The campground has water, flush toilets, and more space than people.

Fruita, the closest town, is at the west end of the monument. **Pancho's Villa** (970-858-9380) restaurant serves breakfast all day and night. The food is great and the service is very friendly. Everybody is welcomed at Pancho's Villa.

Dinamation International Society, the non-profit education and research arm of Dinamation International, is headquartered here. Dinamation is the company that creates most of the animated, robotic creatures you see in the movies. It turns out that Fruita and the surrounding area rest in a valley which contains an almost complete fossil record of the entire age of dinosaurs. The **Fruita Natural History Center,** located in the heart of Fruita, is a great place to see how paleontologists piece together the past.

Having the million-dollar Grand Valley front yard view also means having the 23-mile Rim Rock Drive as a driveway. Built by the Civilian Conservation Corps (CCC), construction began on June 1, 1933. The 23-mile road climbs through hairpins, ducks into tunnels carved into the red rock cliffs, follows natural but isolated benches above the canyon rims, and passes rock cuts sheer enough to slice bread. So rugged is the terrain that just one road fill between the tunnels near the Fruita entrance consumed more than 73,000 cubic yards of earth.

Once on top of the Uncompahgre Plateau Uplift, 2,000 feet above the valley floor, the road is a convoluted creation of asphalt, similar to riding the proverbial snake's back. Built on Kayenta Rock, one of the hardest geologic layer formations, the road has only been paved once, and that was 75 years ago!

Riding the edge with little space between you and purgatory is heaven. Smooth, banked S-turns and overlooks to unusual rock monoliths and canyons are taken at an average speed of 30 mph, with some 10 mph corners. The occasional rock fall is something to keep in mind if not in sight. I've had both deer and coyotes bound across my path. So hold on . . . Okay, you can let go of the handlebars now and get some circulation into those white knuckles.

The ride through **Grand Junction** is uneventful but Route 6 is fruitful, literally, as it passes through orchards of peaches and pears, with many roadside stands for picnic materials. There's no getting around Interstate 70 through Plateau Canyon. It's the only way to go. Route 65 makes up for this and more.

The climb up Grand Mesa starts out with long sweepers hugging Plateau Creek. Plenty of places to air it out and cut tight corners. The north side gets steeper and tighter as it climbs. Travel through four ecological zone changes: pinon-juniper desert canyons, aspen foothills, and finally lily ponds and alpine forest at the 10,893-foot summit. Ride as early in the day as possible if you don't want to find out why the Utes called Grand Mesa "Thunder Mountain." Though it can be hot and dry on the valley floor, a snowball fight could be the game on top.

Grand Mesa, a lava-capped plateau, is the largest flat-top mountain in the world. Unlike many lava flows, there is no volcanic cone. The lava flowed through fissures, forming a cap ranging from 200 to 600 feet thick. The surrounding area, composed of softer rock, eroded over time, leaving Grand Mesa high but not dry. More than 300 stream-fed trout-filled lakes dot the mesa top. Many scenic stops with valley vistas add time to the ride.

The descent off of Grand Mesa is slow and steady, with long sweepers until **Cedaredge.** Cedaredge is in the heart of Surface Creek Valley orchard country. Over 75 percent of Colorado's prized apples grow here. If pressed for time or if the weather is bad at the top, follow Route 63 to Route 50 back to Grand Junction. It's highway and faster.

If a picnic is on your agenda, wait for a spot until you reach the seclusion and undisturbed wilderness of National Forest Service 121's high alpine lakes and meadows. NFS 121 demonstrates the feel of how big and flat

Monoliths at the Colorado National Monument are viewed fom the top down on Rim Rock Drive.

Grand Mesa really is. Although it is a gravel road, it is maintained well enough to dodge the little washboard that there is. An easy road for all bikes but easier if you're not loaded down with the kitchen sink.

Save some energy for the return trip to Rim Rock Drive. The afternoon sun really brings out the colors, the best time for those photo-ops.

For you dual-purpose riders, Lands End Road, at milepost 29 on Route 65, travels west 12 miles along the rim with many scenic vistas to the south and west. Lands End then falls off the mountain for 20 miles and intersects with Route 50 eight miles south of **Whitewater.** When I mean fall off, I mean 55 hair-raising hairpins. Going up this steep, narrow gravel road is even more fun.

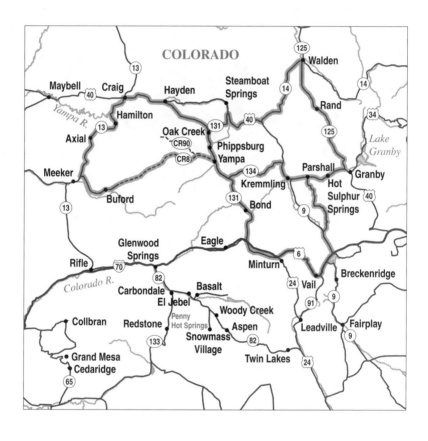

Pass-ing Through Central Colorado

Home base for these loops is free, secluded camping by the Colorado River at **Pioneer Park** in the town of **Hot Sulphur Springs**. Follow the signs to the newly renovated **Hot Sulphur Springs Resort & Spa** (www.hotsulphur-springs.com, 800-510-6235) (off Route 40) over the Colorado River, take first right after the crossing. The dirt road goes back about a mile with many sites to choose from along the river. Plenty of wood and pit toilets for convenience. The river provides natural, albeit cool, showering capabilities or go for a hot springs soak at the spa. The Resort & Spa offers two outside pools and 16 private baths.

The High Way over Ute Pass is spectacular.

Trip 22   Continental Divide Loop

Distance *213 miles*
Highlights *Cross the Continental Divide twice with mountains, mountain curves, and alpine scenery the whole way*

THE ROUTE FROM HOT SULPHUR SPRINGS

Route 40 west to Route 134 west
Route 134 west to Route 131 north
Route 131 north to Route 40 east
Route 40 east to National Forest Service 315
Return National Forest Service 315 to Route 40 east
Route 40 east to Route 14 east
Route 14 east to Route 125 south
Route 125 south to Route 40 west

Kremmling, nestled at the confluence of the Colorado and Blue Rivers, is a small town with a big heart. Hosting barbeques on the town green, it's a strategic stopping place for the annual three-day "Ride The Rockies" bicycle event. If you're using **Hot Sulphur Springs** as home base and approaching from the west, stock up on food, drink, and gas essentials in Kremmling.

Route 134 is a crooked road that travels through the **Arapahoe** and **Routt National Forests.** Gore Pass, at 9,827 feet, is an early challenge on this loop. You can camp at the pass but at 10,000 feet make sure you're in the heat of the summer because snow is always a possibility.

The town of **Oak Creek** is small but has big services like laundry and two restaurants. The **Colorado Bar & Grill** (970-736-0715) has excellent food and daily specials. Route 131 melds with Route 40 just below **Steamboat Springs.** Climb over Rabbit Ears Pass, crossing the Continental Divide, on a civilized, wide, three-laner complete with a climbing lane. Near the crest, take National Forest Service (NFS) 315 to a high alpine meadow NFS campground and access road to the rock formation that inspired the pass's name. In June I had to plow through a few frozen snow streams to get to the view but . . .

Route 14 north plays peekaboo with Grizzly Creek most of the way to Walden. Route 125 gives the swivel-headed rider a 360 degree white-capped mountain panorama. Entering the Arapahoe National Forest, the valley road tightens from sweepers to S-turns to hairpins, topping the

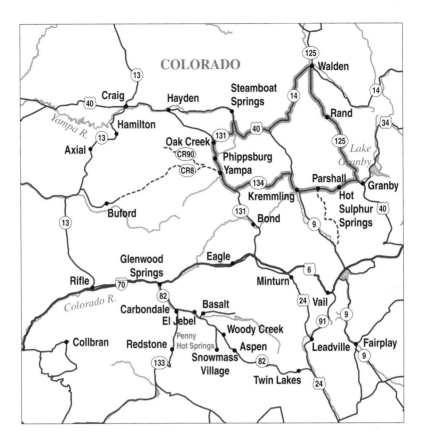

Continental Divide at 9,621-foot Willow Creek Pass. Over the pass, Willow Creek keeps you company to Route 40. Pick up essentials in **Granby.**

Trip 23 Taking the High Way Loop

Distance *166 miles over Ute pass*

THE ROUTE FROM HOT SULPHUR SPRINGS

Route 40 west to Grand County 3 (sign to Williams Fork Reservoir)
Grand County 3 to Forest Road 132 (bear right at all decision points)
Forest Road 132 to Route 9 south
Route 9 south to Interstate 70 west
Interstate 70 west to Route 6 west
Route 6 west to Route 131 north
Route 131 north to Route 134 east
Route 134 east to Route 40 east

Leaving **Hot Sulphur Springs** for **Kremmling** is a Triple-R-R excursion: river, road, and railroad following the same line. Just before the town of Parshall, the Williams Fork branches away from the Colorado River. Take the left onto Grand County 3, and the high way. It's a hard-packed, very little dust-kicking dirt roadbed, easily negotiable by any two-wheeler. This is a remote road through high pristine pine forests dotted with an occasional cabin, with Williams Fork appearing and disappearing like an apparition.

KK's Rib Stand, at the intersection of Routes 6 and 131, is a local hangout for lunch.

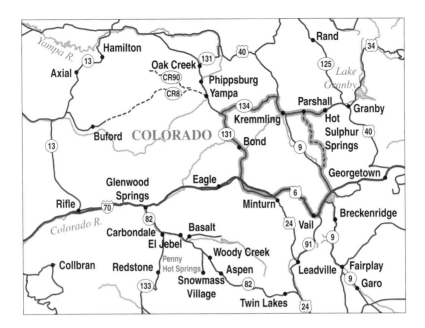

The slow ascent becomes a steep climb to conquer Ute Pass, at 9,524 feet (not to be confused with the other Ute Pass in the "Front Range" section). Cresting Ute Pass, the Blue River Valley, and the Gore Mountain Range unfold ahead of you.

If you're queasy about a little dust, stay on Route 40 west, ride Route 9 south, down Blue River Valley, and pick up the loop at the junction of the two routes above **Silverthorne.** In Siverthorne take Interstate 70 west over Vail Pass, at 10,666 feet, and exit immediately onto Route 6 west in **Dowd.** Route 6 plays peek-a-boo with Interstate 70 while traveling beside the Eagle River and the **Denver and Rio Grand Western Railroad** (D.& R.G.W.R.R. on all those maps).

At the intersection of Routes 6 and 131 stop at **KK's Rib Stand,** a local hangout at lunch time for the truckers. Single beef ribs, hamburgers, and chicken all prepared on the outdoor grill.

Route 131 climbs immediately away from Eagle River and snakes its way to State Bridge. The old bridge used to, and the new bridge does, cross the Colorado River here. At the town of State Bridge is a roadbed back to Kremmling. It is often traveled by the cages (automobiles) for its scenery, which makes for a dusty and washboard ride.

Continue on Route 131 for some great sweepers through sage-spiced highlands, then through **Routt National Forest,** up and over Gore Pass, at 9,527 feet.

Trip 24 Flat Tops Loop

Distance *295 miles*

Highlights *Cross five passes and 57 miles of good solid dirt road through the pristine Flat Tops Mountain Range. Animals everywhere just wondering what you're doing there. Average 30 mph with no concern . . . except for the snow*

THE ROUTE FROM HOT SULPHUR SPRINGS

Route 40 west to Route 134 west

Route 134 west to Route 131 north

Route 131 north to Routt County 131 (Flat Tops Trail sign)

Routt County 131 turns into Rio County 8

Rio County 8 to Route 13 north

When you see "rabbit ears," you'll be approaching Rabbit Ears Pass, near Steamboat Springs on Route 40.

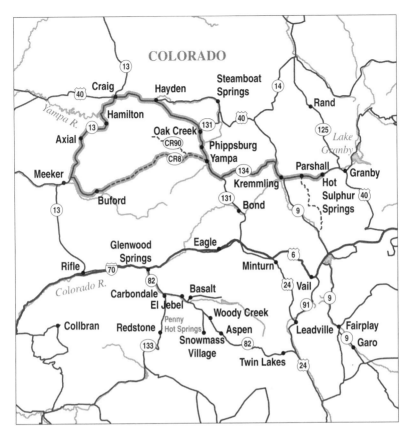

Route 13 north to Route 40 east

Route 40 east to Twenty Mile Road (Routt County 27)

Twenty Mile Road to Route 131 south

Route 131 south to Route 134 east

Route 134 east to Route 40 east

If you are going to spend any time in **Steamboat Springs,** move home base to **Stagecoach State Park** opposite the town of **Oak Creek.** Campsites sitting on the reservoir offer water views and there is a great access road to and from the park.

By now you've become familiar with **Kremmling,** Gore Pass, and this section of **Routt National Forest** (if not, see previous Trips in this region).

The ride over the Flat Tops Mountain Range is a challenging, little-used road through high colorful alpine territory, snaking its way from **Yampa** to **Meeker.**

Allow 2.5 hours for this run, not including stops. The 82-mile ride has approximately 42 miles of unpaved roadbed. The snowpack melts by mid-June; wildlife is the biggest hazard. An elevation change from 6,200 feet to over 10,000 feet causes distinct differences in climate between the valley floors and the two passes you'll cross. The first is Dunckley Pass. At 9,763 feet, the overlook gives a clear view of Pyramid Peak at 11,532 feet. The second is Ripple Creek Pass, which crosses from the Routt National Forest to **White River National Forest** at 10,343 feet.

If you've worked up an appetite over this great ride, stop in downtown Meeker. The **Meeker Hotel & Cafe** (www.themeekerhotel.com, 970-878-5255) has homemade pies that should be rated XXX. Then scoot to **Craig** and pick up the Yampa River on the way to Steamboat Springs.

ALTERNATIVE ROUTE

If you prefer to skip downtown Steamboat, a pleasant way to do that is Twenty Mile Road, a.k.a. Routt County 27. This road is more reminiscent of the rolling hills and twisties of Pennsylvania coal country than alpine Colorado. In fact, there are vast mining operations along the road. Once off Twenty Mile Road the Colorado terrain returns with home base.

You can get home-made X-rated pies at the Meeker Cafe.

FLAT TOPS WITHOUT THE BUTCH WAX

The Flat Tops were formed millions of years ago when molten lava springs broke free and flowed across the land. Following the Ute Indian high summer mountain meadow migratory trail of 1,000 years ago, there are plenty of green valleys, blue rivers, and red rock. The scenery is beautiful enough to need a runaway ramp for the mind.

Forest fires in the nineteenth century opened thousands of acres to aspen growth. After climbing through these fields of aspen, the byway enters the dark timber of spruce. The grayish pall is created by dead standing trees. In the 1940s, an epidemic of the Engelmann spruce beetle devastated the forest. ■

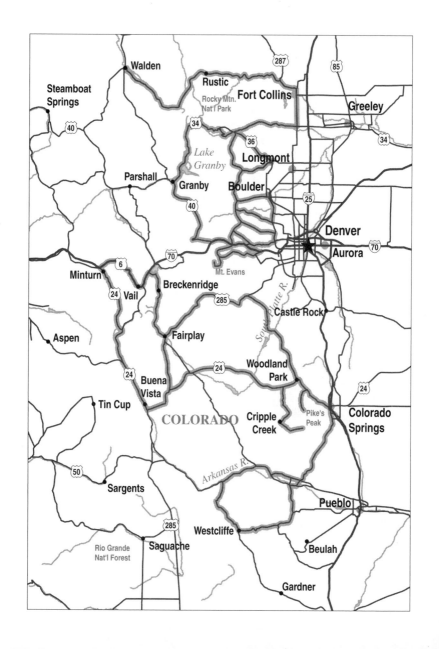

Front Range

The Front Range, or eastern side of the Colorado Rocky Mountains, stretches along the Continental Divide from Raton Pass on the New Mexico border to the Wyoming border. This section takes you from south to north, connecting the region covered by the "Enchantment Land" section (New Mexico), along, up, and over the Rockies into the area of the "West Slope Slalom" section.

The Front Range often serves up afternoon thunderstorms. In fact, the area is number two in the United States for thunderstorm occurrences (see Appendix).

On the Front Range, it can snow at any time!

Trip 25 Highway of Legends Trail

Distance   *82 miles*
Highlights   *A trip where reality is as much fun as the legends. High alpine forests, switchbacks, and curves*

THE ROUTE FROM TRINIDAD
Route 12 north from Trinidad
Route 12 north to Route 160 east to Walsenburg

Legends are the oral history of life. Like the child's game of telephone, each succeeding tale is embellished to reflect another personality. Meeting the National Forest Service Rangers plotting the scenic pullouts and signposts of this 1988-dubbed Scenic Highway of Legends, I asked, "How'd the road get its name?"

He said, "There are an unusual number of legends along these 82 miles, and they're 85 percent truth and 15 percent fiction."

The Highway of Legends has plenty. Maybe you'll create some of your own.

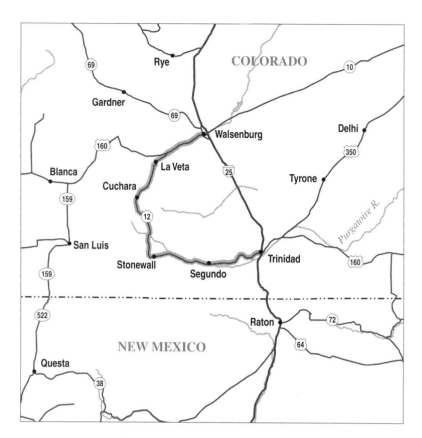

Hesitating, scratching his head a little harder, he continued, "Or is it the other way around?"

Pick up a copy of the legends guide booklet at the county chamber of commerce offices in **Huerfano** (orphan in Spanish), La Veta/Cuchara, or **Trinidad**. Following the highway from south to north, here are some of the legends.

Trinidad Lake State Park (parks.state.co.us/parks/trinidadlake, 719-846-6951) besides being a U.S. Army Corps of Engineers campground with 62 sites, also dams the Purgatoire River. The Purgatoire River (Pur-ga-twa in French, Pur-ga-tory in local) was named many years ago in the time of Coronado and the Spanish Conquistadors' search for the fabled city of gold. Frustrated by the endless search, the leaders of the expedition, Juan Hermana and Francisco Bonilla, fought. Bonilla killed Hermana and forged ahead with the search. He was never seen alive again. Later, their skeletons and armor were found on the river bank. Since they died without the benefit of last rites, they were said to be in purgatory.

West of **Weston**, in full vista splendor, are the Sangre de Cristo Mountains. The early Spanish explorers noticed the mountains turned red with the first rays of dawn—hence the name "Blood of Christ Mountains." Up on the mountains, somewhere near the timberline, is said to be a very rich gold mine. An old legend tells of a prospector who would come off the mountains with a nugget rich enough to buy his entire year's supplies. It is said that he used the reddish color of the morning on the snow to find his mine. Although many have squandered their lives looking, no one else has found the "Gold where the Snow turns to Blood."

Monument Lake is one of several high altitude lakes along the Legends Highway. In the center of the lake, like a monument, breeches a 15-foot rock formation. The rock, as the legend goes, represents two Indian Chiefs, who in ancient times of volcanoes set out from the north and south in search of water for their tribes' survival. When they met they hugged in friendship. Then realizing neither had found water, they wept. The tears formed a lake at their feet. Suddenly one of the volcanoes erupted, covering the two hugging chiefs. The lake remained and water flowed to their people forevermore.

Mooove over!

Downtown Cuchara has everything you really need.

There are many more legends and tall tales to be told. The great news is the highway is a real road filled with enough curves and hairpins, from Trinidad at 6,000 feet to Cuchara Pass at 9,994 feet, to become a legend itself. You can travel between the famed Spanish Peaks, two huge masses of freestanding igneous rock called Wahatoyas (an Indian name meaning the breasts of earth) and the Sangre de Cristo Mountains on the left. Both are snow-capped at least until early June.

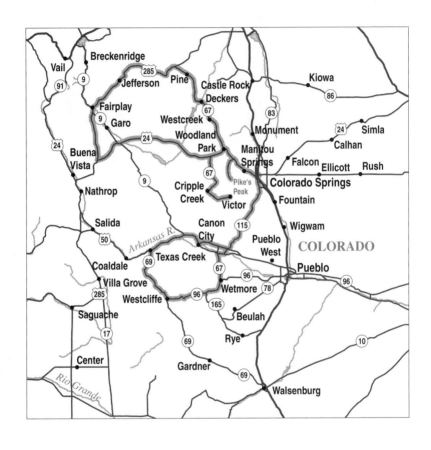

Manitou Springs and Colorado Springs

Home base for these loops is **Manitou Springs.** There are a number of motels and campgrounds in this trendy little village, as well as cafes, shops, and craft demonstrations like glass blowing. The **Garden of the Gods** (www.gardenofgods.com, 719-634-6666) city park is a must. Drive through its magnificent 300 million-year-old red sandstone rock formations. Manitou Springs is located seven miles from downtown **Colorado Springs.**

The daily "Shootout" on Main Street, Cripple Creek, Colorado, is a tame reminder of the wild past.

Trip 26 Pikes Peak & Cripple Creek Loop

Distance *150 miles*
Highlights *Hill climbs, sustained S-turns, off-road gambling, an old ghost town and even older gold mines*

THE ROUTE FROM MANITOU SPRINGS

Route 24 west to Pikes Peak Highway
Pikes Peak Highway to Route 24 west
Route 24 west to Route 67 south (signs to Cripple Creek and Victor)
Route 67 north to Route 24 east

Pikes Peak Highway (www.pikespeakcolorado.com, 800-318-9505) is an unforgettable climb.

Given a choice, go in the morning. The view is less impeded by clouds. On a clear day the curvature of the earth is visible. Afternoon

The best little dirt road in Colorado: heading up Pikes Peak.

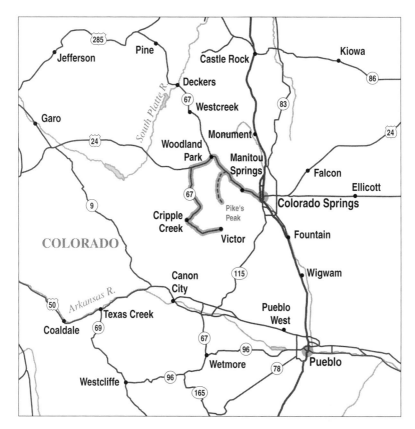

thundershowers are a common occurrence. A comfortable 72 degrees Fahrenheit at the bottom turns into a frigid 35 degrees, without the wind-chill factor, at the top. Bring your woollies, especially warm gloves for the ride. One time I returned to the bottom at 11 a.m. only to find a wind hazard had been posted for motorcycles. The ride takes about two hours depending on traffic and time at the top.

The first seven miles of the 19-mile climb are paved hairpins and S-turns to the Crystal Creek Dam and Reservoir. Just past the reservoir the road turns to what could be the best dirt road in America. The toll pays for the maintenance and, given the climb to be negotiated, is worth the fee.

The toll gate is the starting point for the annual **Pikes Peak Auto Hill Climb.** Usually held on the Fourth of July, the annual event has been running since 1916. Only the Indianapolis 500 has a longer history.

After Crystal Creek Reservoir, where the road turns to roadbed, the climbing really begins. Going from hairpin to hairpin without guardrails, that weak-kneed feeling on the outside of the road sometimes slips into the

 **PEAKING AT PIKE'S**

Lt. Zebulon Montgomery Pike first saw the "great white mountain" in 1806. Dr. Edwin James conquered the mountain 16 years later. The first carriage road was completed in 1888 and the first automobile climbed Pikes Peak in 1901. It'll be hard for you to believe, after the climb, that someone drove up the mountain some one hundred years ago.

Katherine Lee Bates wrote the words to "America the Beautiful" in her room at the Antlers Hotel after a visit to the summit of Pikes Peak in 1893. When you ascend 7,000 feet from Cascade to the summit at 14,110 feet, it's easy to understand the source of her inspiration.   ■

bones (as captain of the ship, we never admit it, but as one captain to another, this is a place where it happens). Stay close to the inside; a lot of cars like to eat two-thirds of very narrow hairpins. First gear is the only gear to worry about. Reaching the summit, both you and the carbs are gasping for air. There is a summit house for warmth, sustenance, and relief.

A couple of tips for climbing and descending the mountain: rubberneck on the way down. If you're water-cooled, run a fast idle for a few minutes at the top to dissipate engine heat. The ranger check at the mid-point of your descent is for brakes, nothing more. If you've got respiratory problems, consider the altitude, dude.

The road to the towns of **Cripple Creek** and **Victor** follows the curvature of the volcanic bowl both are perched on. This 30-mile stretch of beautiful paved road is S-turn after S-turn.

Cripple Creek was the local center of politics, mining, and entertainment at the turn of the century. The town sported two opera houses, 75 saloons, eight newspapers, and a stock exchange. Today, the 75 saloons are replaced with gambling houses. Only a few years in operation, the gaming industry has revived the town, or destroyed it depending who's asked. Money is not the only thing to win here. The Loose Caboose offers a Kawasaki Voyager for a slot machine jackpot.

Non-gamblers will find plenty to do here, too. The casinos offer free drinks and food for a cheap outing. **Wild West Gambling Hall and Brewery** (719-689-4180) makes seven different beers on the premises, and a "one draft free" coupon at the door. I tried the Full Moon Lager. Others include Donkey Beer, Mine Shaft Stout, and Tenderfoot Light. The town sports an antique coal-burning narrow-gauge steam engine for a 45-minute ride, past old gold mines in the nearby hills, a gold mine tour, and shoot-outs right on Main Street every hour or so. Parking is not allowed on Main Street. The way the sheriff gives out tickets, it could be a larger revenue producer than the gaming houses. Stagecoaches and horse drawn buggies do give free rides up and down Main Street.

After Cripple Creek, Route 67 continues past both functioning mines and old mining ghost camps, dead-ending at Victor. Nestled on the south facing slopes of Battle and Squaw Mountains, offering unobstructed views of Pikes Peak and the Sangre de Cristo, San Juan, and Collegiate Mountains, Victor is a neglected jewel which remains almost as it was during the mining boom. The Gold Coin Mine was discovered while excavating the foundation for the hotel in the middle of town. The rigs and mine entrances between the old brick buildings still beckon. In its heyday, over 12,000 people lived in Victor. Lowell Thomas was born and raised here. Jack Dempsey trained in the firehouse and was the local bouncer.

A small caution about the area: loose rocks, weak timbers, and toxic gases make many of the old mines dangerous. Please respect all danger signs.

Don't worry about retracing your steps to Manitou Springs. Familiarity with these roads won't breed contempt.

The finish line at Pikes Peak has a zillion-dollar view as the prize.

Trip 27   Cañon City & Arkansas River Loop

Distance   *216 miles*

Highlights   *Scenic high meadows, running rivers, majestic snow-capped peaks, and a royally deep gorge*

THE ROUTE FROM MANITOU SPRINGS

Route 24 east to Route 115 south (Nevada Ave)

Route 115 south to Route 67 south (signs to Wetmore)

Route 67 south to Route 96 west (signs to Westcliff)

Route 96 west to Route 69 north

Route 69 north to Route 50 east

Route 50 east to Route 115 north (signs to Florence)

Route 115 north to Route 24 west

Royal Gorge Bridge is 1,053 feet above the Arkansas River.

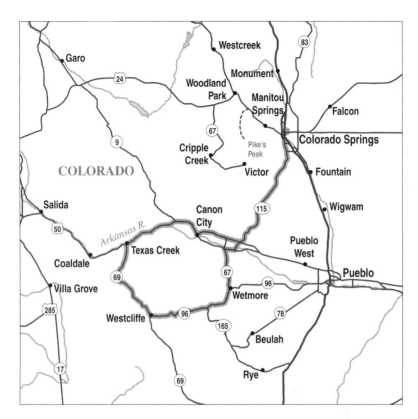

Route 115 is a straight road that narrows with distance from **Colorado Springs**. The **May Natural History Museum** (www.maymuseum-camp-rvpark.com, 800-666-3841), one mile off Route 115, is easy to spot. Take a right by the Hercules Beetle, a giant replica of the nine-inch beetle. The museum, 80 years in the collecting, houses an extensive display of the world's most beautiful and exotic invertebrates from all the tropical areas of the globe. It has 7,000 species of tropical bugs on display. Next door is the **Golden Eagle Ranch Campground,** the only campground I know that advertises it has bugs.

Route 67 crosses the Arkansas River and meanders through the **San Isabel National Forest**. The climb through rough cliff walls near 9,000 feet brings the beauty of the formations quite close to the handlebars. Approaching **Silver Cliff** and **Westcliffe** (anyone's guess as to where one ends and the other begins), the Sangre de Cristo Range looms dead ahead. With six peaks over 14,000 feet, and names like Kit Carson, Challenger, and Crestone Needle, it's hard to keep both eyes on the road. Such majesty is hypnotic.

Fabulous snow-covered peaks surround you on this loop.

The trance is broken when the road looks like it's going to hit the proverbial brick wall. A hard right onto Route 69 veers beside the mountain range and runs through high meadow in the shadow of these peaks, passing ranch after ranch for 25 beautiful miles. Intersect with the Arkansas River and Route 50 at Texas Creek. For 26 glorious miles the road, river, and railroad (a Triple R-R route) all parallel.

Signs for **Royal Gorge Bridge** (www.royalgorgebridge.com, 888-333-5597), at 1,053 feet above the Arkansas River, the world's highest suspension bridge, start to dot the landscape. It is a theme park with trams across and down the gorge. The approach road to the southern entrance is seven miles of challenging narrow asphalt ribbon.

Rejoining Route 50 east, a small sign announcing "Skyline Drive, next left" appears on the approach to **Cañon City**. Skylines with drives are always intriguing combinations. Hang a left and run up an eight-foot-narrow, one-lane ridge road. With 800-foot dropoffs on both sides, this 1.5-mile road overlooking Cañon City and the Sangre de Cristo Range is great practice for ridge road rattles. At the bottom, hang a right on 5th Avenue and a left on Route 50 to rejoin the loop back to home base.

Skyline Drive is no place to get the wobblies. With 800-foot dropoffs, this 1.5-mile road is great practice for ridge road rattles.

The May Museum is the only place I've seen that advertises they have bugs.

Trip 28   Manitou Springs to Buena Vista Loop

Distance *260 miles*
Highlights *Everything from three scenic high passes to tight twisties, beside the Platte River*

THE ROUTE FROM MANITOU SPRINGS

Route 24 west to Route 67 north
Route 67 north to County Route 126 north
County Route 126 north to Route 285 south
Route 285 south to Route 24 east *
Route 24 east to Route 67 south
Return Route 67 north to Route 24 east

* ALTERNATE ROUTE

Knock off 18 miles by grabbing Route 9 south at Fairplay or grab Route 24
     west and set up a new home base in Buena Vista. For a description of
     Buena Vista and a new home base, see the Banana Valley Region.

The climb out of **Manitou Springs** begins before the engine warms. Once on Route 67, the next 65 miles confirms the choice to ride a bike instead of drive a cage. The Platte River provided a backdrop for the engineers who designed this river-hugging road. After **Deckers**, National Forest Service campgrounds and scenic pullouts dot the entire road.

The road from **Buffalo Creek** to **Pine** narrows even more, until bronco busting a snake comes to mind. It's everything a motorcyclist desires in a road: curves, scenery, and little traffic, packed into one. After a road like this hunker down to Route 285, with wide sweepers and climbs, up and down Kenosha Pass at 10,001 feet and Red Hill Pass at 9,993 feet, into South Park. South Park is a broad valley covering more than 900 square miles. Those snow-capped 14,000-foot mountains of the Continental Divide are the Mosquito and Park Ranges.

Fairplay, a mining district once known as Fairplay Diggings, was established in 1859. The name came from the opinion that every one would have an equal chance to stake a claim. Other names for the town were Platte City and South Park City. **South Park City** (www.southparkcity.org, 719-836-2387), on the outskirts of Fairplay, is a 32-building, 19th century museum depicting an authentic Colorado mining town.

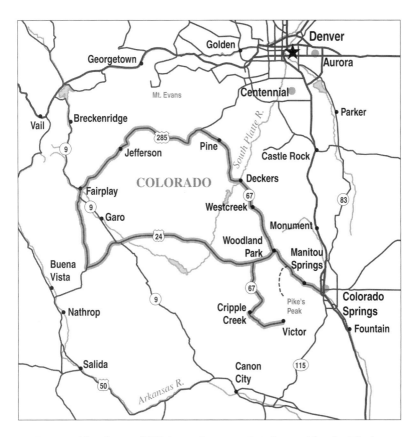

Route 24 heads over Wilkinson Pass at 9,502 feet and by the **Florissant Fossilbeds National Monument,** before heading into gambling country.

Banana Valley Region

Called the Banana Valley because of its shape, the Upper Arkansas Valley is also "home of the 14ers" with more peaks over 14,000 feet than any other place in Colorado—15 in the Sawatch Range alone. It is the mightiest range in the 3,000-mile stretch between New Mexico and the Canadian Rockies. The Sawatch Range also contains four of Colorado's five highest mountains. Bordered by this part of the Continental Divide on the west and the 9,000-foot Mosquito Range on the east, Banana Valley is a great place to explore.

This is St. Elmo's Town Hall, 20 miles from our home base.

Along the Arkansas River are many campgrounds. **Chaulk Creek Campground** (800-395-8337) in **Nathrop,** with full amenities, is the most secluded. Primitive camping can be had along the road to St. Elmo, and you'll find motels in **Buena Vista.**

St. Elmo, on the National Register of Historic Places, is one of the best-preserved ghost towns in Colorado. High in the mountains, 20 miles from home base, St. Elmo was established in the 1870s. Within ten years there were 50 mines and 2,000 people living in town. In the 1930s the gold had run out and the residents with it. Many of the original buildings remain and are in remarkably good shape. The town can be reached by taking County Road 162 off Route 285 in Nathrop. Bring a bathing suit, **Mount Princeton Hot Springs** is along the way.

Buena Vista is the first town on the ride up the valley. Called by the locals Buenie (Bwu-nee), there are two places to check out. The first place is the **Loback's Bakery** (719-395-2978). Originally built in 1879, it has been a bakery all its life. The Braun family operated the bakery from the turn of the century to the 1930s when the Loback family took it over. The Lobacks still own it today. Between 7:30 and 9:00 in the morning, everyone from the mayor to the local ranchers is having a cup of java and a sweet something. The breads are excellent too, for that upcoming picnic.

Here's the morning hangout at Buena Vista.

Bring a bathing suit and have a soak in the Mt. Princeton Hot Springs.

The second place, if you're a railroad buff, is the **Buena Vista Heritage Museum** (719-395-8458). On the second floor, the Buena Vista Model Railroad Society has created an elaborate model of the railroads that operated in the valley from the late 1800s to the 1920s.

Trip 29   Peeling the Banana Loop

Distance *173 miles*
Highlights *Through the valley, climbing into mining history, over ski country, beside the tallest mountains in Colorado*

THE ROUTE FROM NATHROP

Route 285 north to Route 24 west
Route 24 west to Interstate 70 east
Interstate 70 east to Route 9 south
Route 9 south to Route 285 south
Route 285 south merges with Route 24 west
Route 24 west/Route 285 south to Route 285 south

Touring Route 24, known as the "Highway of the Fourteeners" because it passes a total of ten 14,000 foot peaks, is an Ivy League experience without the tuition bill. The Collegiate Peaks—Harvard, Yale and Princeton at 14,420, 14,196, and 14,197 feet respectively—form the center of the Sawatch Range. Near Mount Harvard is Mount Columbia at 14,073 feet.

Tabor Opera House, Leadville, Colorado, was built out of love and silver.

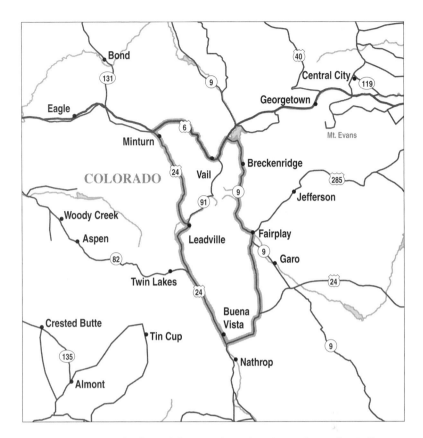

Buena Vista sits at the foot of these peaks and each year hosts the Collegiate Peaks 100-mile Enduro Run.

S-turning upstream beside the mighty Arkansas River, peek over the edge and watch rafters heading downstream. The Arkansas River is the most rafted river in Colorado and the section between Buena Vista and **Leadville** is the most challenging. Just before the town of Leadville is Mount Elbert, at 14,433 feet, highest of all the Rocky Mountains and the second highest peak in the contiguous 48 states.

Leadville (a.k.a. Cloud City), at 10,152 feet, and the Leadville mining district have a history rich in storybook romance, and fortunes made and lost. All are equal to the best romance fiction. The most famous and tragic story begins with **Horace Austin Warner Tabor.**

"Unsinkable" **Molly Brown** was another famous resident of Leadville. On board the Titanic in 1912 when it sank, she earned her nickname "Unsinkable" with her fabled indefatigable nature, which kept the people in Lifeboat #6 alive.

➡ **LEADVILLE LOVE**

Horace Austin Warner Tabor arrived in California Gulch, Kansas (later renamed Colorado) Territory in May of 1860. Stricken with gold fever, he soon made his money "mining the miners." He opened a general store, and became Leadville's first mayor. He grubstaked a couple of miners, to the tune of $14. They discovered the huge Little Pittsburg mine and turned Tabor into one of the territory's richest silver barons overnight. Enter Elizabeth Bonduel McCourt Doe, 25 years old and 24 years his junior.

The courtship, Tabor's divorce, and his marriage to "Baby Doe," scandalized all of America. Society spurned the couple, but she continued to help Tabor spend his millions in a lifestyle befitting the rich and famous. Like all markets, what goes up must come down. No one anticipated the Silver Panic of 1893.

The panic wiped out Tabor. To the amazement of those who called her a gold digger (or silver digger), Baby Doe sold her possessions to help support him. He died in April, 1899. Baby Doe lived in abject poverty for the rest of her life, true to her legendary promise never to sell the mine.   ∎

Other heroes learned to stay alive in the high country snows. Between Leadville and **Vail,** just north of 10,424-foot Tennessee Pass, the U.S. Army formed the 10th Mountain Division. Camp Hale, named for Brigadier General Irving Hale, was built in seven months. Four hundred buildings housed 15,000 men between 1942 and 1945. Dressed in camouflage white, they became known as the Invisible Men of the 10th. They, along with 5,000 mules and 200 K9 Corps dogs, trained in 15 feet of snow and minus 35 degree weather. The 10th saw overseas action in the Italian Alps. Special training stopped at Camp Hale in 1965. The area is now used by the 10th Mountain Division Hut Association, and provides 12 huts for shelter to hikers and mountain bikers.

Interstate 70 is the only interstate I recommend other than as a necessary evil. Over Vail Pass, at 10,666 feet, the super slab feels small, dwarfed by the landscape surrounding it. It gets even better heading toward Denver, but that's another story, so exit at **Frisco** (don't let anybody from San Francisco hear you say that) or if you want extra miles, incorporate the Route 91 run into the loop.

Off of Interstate 70, before Frisco, the extra 48 mile round-tripper adds the 11,318-foot Freemont Pass to the notches on your belt. The damming of Tenmile Creek near the pass flooded three towns, including the highest Masonic Temple in the United States. A commemorative plaque at the turnout is a good excuse to stop and enjoy a snow-capped panorama backgrounding the reservoir. At this elevation it can snow anytime.

Looking for the town of **Climax** is frustrating. It doesn't exist except for the mine and a name on a map.

Highway 9 from Frisco to **Breckenridge** parallels the Blue River. Breckenridge is an 1859 mining town turned Victorian ski resort. Gold was discovered in 1859 and the largest gold nugget in Colorado was found there 28 years later. Nicknamed "Tom's Baby," the 1887 find weighed in at a hefty 156 ounces or 13 pounds (Troy weight). The rocks piled high along the river banks are remnants of the early 1900s search for gold using dredging barges.

Climb up and over the Continental Divide at 11,541-foot Hoosier Pass. It's a great narrow, well-paved, two-laner climb up and then down into **Alma** and the intersection of Route 24 in Fairplay.

From Fairplay, home base is close. One mile after cresting Trout Creek Pass at 9,346 feet, the pointed summit of Mt. Princeton first appears followed in succession to the right by Mounts Yale and Columbia. Three-quarters of a mile further, just before the highway breaks left, is the sharp peak of Mount Harvard, third highest in the Rockies. To the right are Mounts Missouri, Belford, and Oxford, all higher than 14,000 feet. Once the entire range unfurls, a scenic overlook is provided on the right. Stop for a panoramic view, and a good lesson in history and geology.

Golden Canyons Region

Golden may be named for its aspens, its early prospecting days, or maybe its Coors beer. I'd stake a claim for its golden canyons and ridge roads. Home base for these three trips is **Golden Gate Canyon State Park** (parks.state.co.us/parks/goldergatecanyon, 303-582-3707). At 9,000 feet, this park offers two different styles of camping. The higher primitive campground (tents only) offers unique sites nestled in pine, aspen, and sculptured rock. The lower one offers showers, conveniences, and large pine-forested sites. The closest provisions are in **Nederland.**

A word of caution: the Colorado State Park system has a quirk that can make the unaware biker a victim of bureaucracy. There is now a reservation system covering all 40 state parks. The reservation list does not come out until the Thursday before the weekend, so if you arrive before Thursday, you may have to break and make camp twice. If you arrive before Thursday without reservations and plan to stay through the weekend, announce it when you register and ask the ranger for one of the "hold sites." It usually isn't the best site available, but it's better than breaking camp in the rain, like I did, with more than 100 other sites empty. Expletive deleted! Grrrrrrr!

Trip 30   Top of the Paved Continent Loop

Distance   *200 miles*

Highlights   *Zigzag through turns, canyons, creeks, lakes, rivers, and three life zones to the highest paved North American road. At the end, you'll have hot sidewalls and cool bottoms*

THE ROUTE FROM GOLDEN GATE CANYON STATE PARK

Route 119 west to Route 279 south

Route 279 south to right on Business I-70 west

Business I-70 west to Route 103 south

Route 103 south to Route 5 south

Return Route 5 north to Route 103 south

Route 103 south to Route 74 north

Route 74 north to Interstate 70 west

Interstate 70 west to Route 6 east

This is literally the top of the paved world in North America—over 14,000 feet.

Route 6 east to Route 58/93 north (follow Route 93 north)

Route 93 north to left on Golden Gate Canyon Road (turns into 70 Road west)

70 Road west to Route 46 west

Route 46 west to Route 119 east

Route 119 east to Route 72 east

Route 72 east to Route 93 north

Route 93 north to Route 119 west

Route 119 west to entrance of Golden Gate Canyon State Park and home base

Route 119 is nicknamed The Peak to Peak Highway. Although there are plenty of mountain peaks surrounding the area, like the highway, most are anonymous. Heading west (it feels south) on Route 119 from home base is only a warm-up, albeit one of the best warm-ups, for a ride.

Entering **Black Hawk** and starting just above **Central City** is Route 279. It's obscure through Central City, so if you miss it, just ask in downtown for the "Oh My Gawd Highway." The name is far more intimidating than the road. Even shiny cruiser weights can do this one-time stagecoach road. Being a backroad, it doesn't appear on maps, but is an excellent dirt road that cuts through Virginia Canyon and into Idaho Springs from the backside. Along the way are many abandoned mines honeycombing the hillsides. The green hillsides dotted with the sandy beige old mine dumps and shaft houses conjure up an army of giant ants building their colonies. Some of the road gets narrow, but with little traffic it's not a biggie.

The next stop is a biggie, really the highest. The ride to Mount Evans is a climb to 14,260 feet. This is the top of the paved world—or at least North America, depending on who's talking. This is an adjustment in altitude and attitude. Cool all the time, snow any time, this 28-mile roundtripper passes lakes named Echo (go ahead, try it), at 10,600 feet, and Summit, at 12,830 feet. The eight-foot snow banks mean snowball fights in July. The **Mount Evans Crest House,** built between 1940 and 1941, sits at 14,260 feet. With views of the Continental Divide and the Front Range, the top of Mount Evans redefines the word vista.

"Oh My Gawd" Highway sounds more intimidating than it is. Even big cruisers can handle the hard-packed gravel surface.

You'll have a chance to meet new friends along the way. Here, a group of locals take a refreshing stroll.

Back down Route 5 at the junction of Route 103 is the **Echo Lake Lodge** (303-567-2138), a friendly place to warm the cockles from a cold ride. The fun heats up again riding through **Pike National Forest,** up and over Squaw Pass at 9,807 feet. With the circulation returning to the extremities, start warming up for the canyon rides.

Begin with Clear Creek Canyon, 15 miles beside Clear Creek, then through 13 miles of Golden Gate Canyon, and finally, end run down the 20 miles of Coal Creek Canyon. Just when the forearms need a breather from all that countersteering comes Route 93 north.

Route 93 tries to be a challenging road to **Boulder** but the DPW smoothed out many of the curves and left a few sweepers of what could have been. Boulder is a manageable city of good food, diverse lifestyles, and stunning beauty. It also appears to be an enlightened city, given all the "motorcycle only" parking areas near the promenades.

Trip 31 Rocky Mountain High Loop

Distance *184 miles*

Highlights *The finest views in the United States. Rocky Mountain National Park is a must-see. One of the five most visited parks in the country, it is always crowded, so relax and enjoy the extra rubbernecking time the traffic gives you. The roads to and from the park are nothing to sneeze at, either. Plan at least a full day.*

THE ROUTE FROM GOLDEN GATE CANYON STATE PARK

Route 119 east to Route 72 west
Route 72 west to Route 7 west
Route 7 west to Route 34 west
Route 34 west to Route 40 east
Route 40 east to Interstate 70 east
Interstate 70 east to Route 6 east (left lane exit)
Route 6 east to Route 119 east

Vistas such as this are in abundance on Trail Ridge Road, Rocky Mountain National Park.

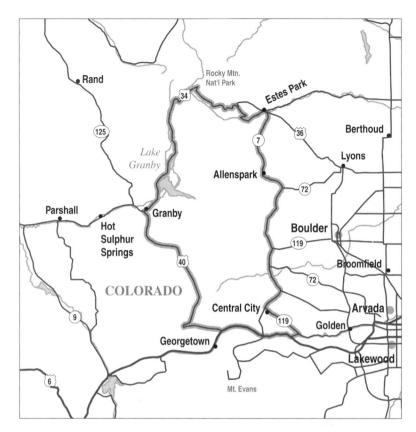

Like an overture to a symphony, the routes to **Rocky Mountain National Park** prepare the rider for what's ahead. As mentioned, Route 119 is nicknamed the Peak to Peak Highway. Renaming it the Many Peaks Highway would be more accurate. Wandering through the **Roosevelt National Forest,** Routes 119, 72, and 7 have many peaks and valleys. All are conquered with tight curves, lots of hairpins, sideways esses, and cresting turns. Your first crest to valley is entering **Nederland.**

Nederland, a small mountain town with a history of shipping and distribution during the gold rush days, offers the closest grocery, gas, and eateries to **Golden Gate Canyon State Park.** The Mining Company Nederland of the Hague bought the mill and surrounding mining properties sitting on Middle Boulder Creek, hence the town's European name.

Nederland is also a legendary music town with many venues. The **Pioneer Inn** (303-258-7733) offers a range of pub grub, live music Thursday through Sunday, and a full complement of local color. It's worth a toe-tapping stop.

This is the former home of Enos Mills, "father" of Rocky Mountain National Park.

Peaceful Valley, reflecting the road as much as the terrain, is the next bottoming-out spot. Just after **Meeker Park** is the cabin of **Enos Mills,** the naturalist, writer, and conservationist who is known as the father of Rocky Mountain National Park.

Mills, declaring, "The Rockies are not a type, but an individuality, singularly rich in mountain scenes which stirs one's blood and which strengthen and sweeten life," began a campaign for the preservation of the area. He succeeded in 1915 when Rocky Mountain National Park (www.nps.gov/romo, 970-586-1206) was created. Rocky Mountain National Park is a spectacular wilderness ranging from deep canyons to alpine meadows to craggy mountain peaks, 76 of which are above 12,000 feet. The park's 415 square miles straddle the Continental Divide, where snow melt and rain flow west to the Pacific or southeast to the Gulf of Mexico.

Trail Ridge Road, cutting through and riding the top of the park, is one of the great alpine highways in the United States. Connecting Estes Park with Grand Lake, it takes three or four hours to cover the "Roof of the Rockies." It can be crowded in the summer months. On a clear day, average visibility is 83 miles, so relax and enjoy the 50-mile road ride rising to

12,183 feet above sea level. Trail Ridge Road is usually open from Memorial Day to Mid-October depending on the weather. It snows every month of the year here. Full-dresser applies to rider and scooter alike.

One-third of the park and 11 miles of Trail Ridge Road are above tree line and tundra. The tundra is a harsh world where five-year-old plants are smaller than your fingernail, and foot traffic takes hundreds of years to repair. The park offers a variety of plant life, varying with the altitude and sunlight. Open stands of ponderosa pine and juniper grow on the south-facing slopes; cooler north slopes are home to Douglas fir. Stream-side are blue spruces intermixed with lodgepole pines. Wildflowers paint the meadows with a full pallete of colors. More than a quarter of the plants that grow in the upper regions of the park are also native to the Arctic.

After crossing Milner Pass at 10,758 feet, my favorite picnic spot appears on the right. If the snow has melted, Lake Irene is a serene spot away from the crowd. From Lake Irene, Trail Ridge Road slowly descends through Farview Curve, passing the Colorado River headwaters, Never Summer Ranch, and the Kawuneeche Visitor Center before leaving the park for Grand Lake.

Grand Lake, seen from the veranda of Grand Lake Lodge, is worth a sneak peek even if you can't afford to stay at the lodge.

Grand Lake, named after the county it's in, is the largest natural lake in Colorado. It was formed by the Colorado River, which before the turn of the century was called the Grand River. As the river flowed south, it created the canyon which also bears its name.

The Utes controlled the area around Grand Lake in the early 1800s, fighting off the marauding Cheyenne and Arapahoe who traveled from the Eastern Plains to these rich hunting grounds. The Ute, to protect their women and children during a battle, would float their families onto the lake on a raft. One unfortunate time, a storm with high winds capsized the raft, drowning the entire village. The grieving Utes named the waters Spirit Lake, left the area, and never returned.

It's hard to see from the road, but follow the signs (it's a left) to **Grand Lake Lodge** (www.grandlakelodge.com, 970-627-3967). An international clientele enjoys the lodge's full-length veranda view of Grand Lake and Shadow Mountain Reservoir, backdropped by verdant, tree-covered mountains. It is sometimes called "Colorado's Favorite Front Porch." Three vintage cars and a directional signpost with mileage to Rio de Janeiro, Tokyo, San Jose (Argentina, Chile, or Costa Rica, but definitely not California), and other international destinations sit outside the office. A view worth the effort and if you can afford the lodge, it's a peaceful, luxurious splurge.

Peck House, in Empire, is the oldest hotel in Colorado still in operation.

Back on Route 34, the ride stays on high alpine meadow until the T-intersection at Granby. Hang a left and follow the Fraser River into the ski resort of **Winter Park**. From the ski resort, Route 40 climbs and climbs up to Berthoud Pass at 11,315 feet. Crest the pass and descend into the small mining town of **Empire**.

The **Peck House** (www.thepeckhouse.com, 303-569-9870) in Empire is the state's oldest hotel still in operation. It's a genteel place to have a cool drink on the veranda overlooking the Empire Valley. Empire is also home to the original Hard Rock Cafe, on Main Street a.k.a. Route 40. It is easy to see that the sign and structure predate all those T-shirts. It closes at 2 p.m. and serves breakfast.

At Empire, merge with Interstate 70, and exit left onto Route 6 for a 15-mile tight, twisting, enveloped-by-towering-cliffs ride along Clear Creek Canyon. The existing roadway is built on the roadbed of yesterday's trains, which brought gold seekers up to the mining camps of **Black Hawk** and **Central City**. The last freight train ran up the canyon on May 5, 1941. It was only after the tracks were pulled and the canyon walls blasted that the road was built.

Route 6 also passes through three tunnels. Tunnel No. 2 is 1,168 feet long and the second longest in Colorado. The longest is Eisenhower Tunnel on Interstate 70, 8,941 feet long.

Route 119 east is 10 miles from the gambling towns of Central City and Black Hawk. In gold mining days these two towns were nicknamed the "richest square mile on earth." Central City, like Cripple Creek, has renovated Victorian buildings packed with gamblers and slot machines. Central City also boasts a few firsts: the first gold strike in Colorado, at Gregory Gulch by **John H. Gregory,** and the first Stetson Hat, produced in the 1860s by **John B. Stetson.**

Trip 32 Cache la Poudre Trail

Distance *230 miles*

Highlights *Canyon roads, cut by creeks and rivers that never flowed in a straight line. Mated to these canyon carvers are smooth-walled, river-hugging roads, including the only designated "wild and scenic river" in Colorado*

THE ROUTE FROM GOLDEN GATE CANYON STATE PARK

Route 119 east to Route 72 west *

Route 72 west to Route 7 east

Route 7 east to Route 36 north

Route 36 north to Route 34 east

Route 34 east to Route 287 north

Route 287 north to Route 14 west (left on Mulberry Street in Fort Collins)

The Cache la Poudre was the first river in Colorado to be officially designated "Wild and Scenic."

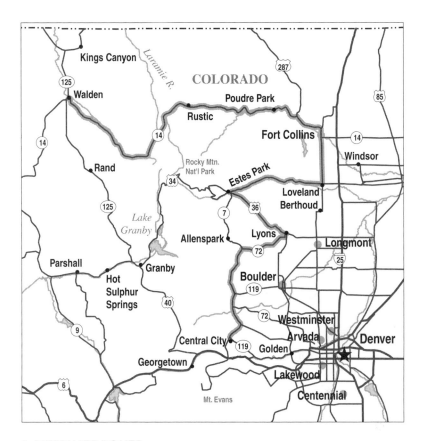

* ALTERNATE ROUTE

Route 119 east to Route 36 (turn left at 28th Street in Boulder). It's an alternative way to Estes Park via a valley road along the foothills outside of Boulder.

This is canyon country. The height of the canyon walls, the straining to see around the next curve, and the quick look at the rivers make you feel like one of those back window gooney head bobbers with brake light eyes. Be prepared for an aching neck.

Boulder Canyon and Big Thompson Canyon are delightful appetizers to begin this full course canyon meal. Follow Boulder Creek, out of the university town of the same name, with twists and turns tantalizing the senses and whetting the appetite. Leaving **Estes Park** via Route 34 east, travel the Big Thompson Canyon beside the Big Thompson River, happy to be on sticky tires for the little unnerving slides on slick hot-day-crack-filled tar. In 1984, the Big Thompson received 11 inches of rain in less than five hours.

The Southwest offers superb riding, like here on Rim Rock Drive in the Colorado National Monument.

Normally a couple of feet in depth, the river rose to 20 feet within hours, scouring the canyon of anything in its path, and washing away 139 people and countless homes. It is easy to imagine how the river could rear its head for this devastation, because of the narrowness of the canyon walls and the water level nearly to the road even during normal times.

Route 287 to **Fort Collins** is motel city. Plenty to choose from and a full complement of retail stores and restaurants to go with them. It is a small price to pay for the gourmet and gourmand blend of asphalt spices being cooked by Route 14.

The outstanding 101-mile Cache la Poudre Scenic Byway demonstrates Colorado at its best. Steeped in local history of mountain men, pioneering, and early stagecoach days, the Cache la Poudre (French for "hide the powder") Wild and Scenic River is the first and only river in Colorado to earn this national designation. The Byway runs from Ted's Place, just west of Fort Collins, to **Walden** in the North Park Region, just below Wyoming.

The **Roosevelt National Forest** surrounds the river and Route 14 literally cuts through the heart of it. Baldwin Tunnel, bored in the fall of 1916, eliminated the need for traveling the old North Park Stage Line road to **Livermore** and then down **Pingree Hill** to **Rustic.**

Offering tourists and wanderers a wide range of places to stay, Rustic is an apt description of the town. Campgrounds, rustic cabins, lodges, and fancy inns abound.

After Rustic, Route 14 leads to the Big Narrows, a forbidding granite chasm made passable by convict labor blasting through the rock in 1919. Old Man's Face (Profile Rock) is on the left, 1.7 miles past the Poudre Canyon fire station. There are several parking areas to grab that obligatory tourist shot.

After Chambers Lake, the climb through Cameron Pass peaks at 10,276 feet. Next, Route 14 slowly descends into **Gould** at 8,000 feet and, while paralleling the Michigan River, shoots into Walden. Staying above 6,000 feet through mountains reaching over 12,000 feet and then easing back down to 8,000 feet, it's easy to understand why the Cache la Poudre Byway area is referred to by the locals as the "hideaway where the natives play."

Walden is a crossroads town. Head north to Wyoming through the pristine North Park area on Route 125 and close the book. Head west on Route 14 to **Steamboat Springs,** through the Rabbit Ears Mountains and Pass, or south, on Route 125 beside the Never-Summer Range, and set up a new home base in **Hot Sulphur Springs** (see Trip 22 in the "West Slope Slalom" section). Steamboat Springs is covered in that section too.

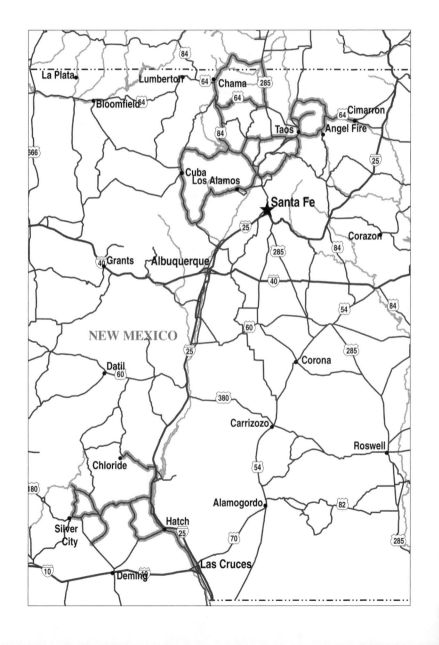

Enchantment Land

Many people think of New Mexico as a land of desert. It's true that the state is characterized by arid deserts to the south and east, but the central region features the Rio Grande River, its valleys and lakes formed by damming, and the north and west boast towering mountains, deep gorges, and verdant forests. This varied landscape, coupled with the state's status as the sunniest place in the United States, means "let the good times roll."

Rich in heritage, New Mexico is where the past and present live side by side. Explore ancient civilizations, Native American pueblos, quaint Hispanic villages, and modern skyline cultures. The peoples' influences vary as much as the terrain. New Mexico's Pueblo tribes share their ancestry with the Hopi, being direct descendants of the Anasazi civilization. The 19 Pueblo settlements are found from just south of **Albuquerque** to **Taos.** Hispanic influence began with Don Juan de Oñate's colonization of the valley in 1598. The first Spanish capital in the United States was founded six miles north of Española at San Juan Pueblo. Anglo influences were frontiersmen and trappers, the most famous of these being **Kit Carson.**

This section focuses, from south to north, on the central and northern regions of New Mexico.

Connect with the "Hanging on the Mogollon Rim" section by heading north on Route 180 from the City of Rocks home base. The "2 x Four Corners" section connects by heading west via Trip 47. And the "Front Range" section connects from this section, via Trip 38, by heading north from **Cimarron** via Trip 25.

➡ FLAME ON

The green chile is one of New Mexico's official state vegetables (the other being frijoles, or pinto beans). In fact, the state leads the nation in chile growing. Hatch is the self-proclaimed "Chili Capital of the World."

Most of the chiles grown in New Mexico are descendants of the chiltepines, the hottest peppers known. They contain huge amounts of capsaicins, the odorless, colorless, flavorless chemicals that give chiles their burn. ∎

Cities of Rock

Home base for these loops is **City of Rocks State Park** (www.newmexico-.org/place/loc/parks/page/DB-place/place/537.html, 505-536-2800). The two-mile entrance from Route 61, climbing gently over high plain, gives no clue to the incongruity cresting the hill reveals: one square mile of huge boulders plunked in the middle of nowhere. Formed over 30 million years ago by rapidly cooling and congealing volcanic ash, the rain-worn and wind-carved rocks resemble city houses, roads, and towers.

The windmills, 56 campsites, and other structures built ingeniously among the rocks blend so inconspicuously that the designers surely deserve a tip of the helmet. Sites 54, 53, 50, and 4 provide the best protection from the southwesterlies. If your gang is organizing an outing and games like Capture the Flag or Hide and Seek are on the agenda, look no further than this playground.

Home base is City of Rocks State Park. Little known and private you can play here for a long time.

Trip 33   Gila Cliff Dwellings Loop

Distance *170 miles*
Highlights *Tight S-turns, hairpins, and climbs through deep river-carved canyons to vistas on cliff-hugging sweepers*

THE ROUTE FROM CITY OF ROCKS STATE PARK

New Mexico Route 61 north to Route 152 west
Route 152 west to Route 35 north
Route 35 north to Route 15 north
Route 15 north to Gila Cliff Dwellings National Monument
Return Route 15 south to Route 152 east
Route 152 east to Route 61 south
Route 61 south to home base

Starting out from **City of Rocks State Park,** Route 61 and Route 35 follow the Mimbres River Valley. The well-marked roads climb 45 miles through Mimbres Canyon. Staying at river-level, the sweepers stretch from 25 to 55 mph. When the road branches away from the Mimbres River, the climb becomes steeper and signs for Lake Roberts start to appear. Fed by the Gila (HEE-la) River, the lake provides a scenic backdrop for picture or picnic.

Just beyond Lake Roberts, joining the Gila River on the left, is the Route 15 intersection. The Middle and West forks of the Gila River seem to fade to streams as the road pulls up and away, hugging the cliff wall. Cresting 10 miles before the cliff dwellings, the steady third gear (sometimes second) descent allows vista viewing.

Gila Cliff Dwellings National Monument (www.nps.gov/gicl, 505-536-9461), another city of rocks, was last occupied more than 700 years ago. The earliest inhabitants found the nearby creek a dependable year-round source of water. They lived in seven naturally formed caves, six of which contain ruins of these prehistoric (because they left no written record) dwellers. Perhaps 40 to 50 people lived in the 40 rooms from about 1280 to the early 1300s, tilling soil and hunting small game.

Pueblo is a Spanish term applied to Southwestern Indians who built communal houses, farmed, and made pottery. This area was occupied by the Pueblo Indians of the Mogollon (mug-ee-YOWN) culture. Today's Northern Pueblo Indians are direct descendants of these people.

The original inhabitants used stone tools to level bedrock floors, then

they plastered the floors with mud for a hard, even surface. The vigas (VEE-gahs), large beams for the roof, were cut with stone axes and fire. They supported smaller poles and finally, a mud roof.

The dwellings were later used by the Apaches who came into this area many years later, but the first recorded visit by a European was credited to archeologist-historian **Adolph Bandelier** in 1884.

Retracing Route 15 about 12 miles south, a quarter of a mile of rough dirt road leads to **Gila Hot Springs** (small sign on Route 15). The water leaves the ground at 165 degrees Fahrenheit. To accommodate everybody, the water flows through three shallow cooling pools. For a small fee, the visitor gets primitive campsites with his and her pit toilets, fishing, and soaking rights, opposite a huge canyon wall on the Gila River.

After the intersection of Route 35, Route 15 south blossoms into a series of fourth, third, second, and occasionally first gear hairpins through pine and cedar forest. Choosing this path provides the most climbing miles.

Silver City is a good place to gas up, buy provisions, or eat the mother lode at **Kountry Kitchen** (505-388-4512). Route 152 east, past the Santa Rita Open-Pit Copper Mine, Silver City's main source of income, is a wide stretch of highway back to home base.

Trip 34 Black Range Loop

Distance *205 miles*
Highlights *Hairpins and switchbacks, climbs to 8,000-foot vistas, and curves through high plains, wide-open range country, and hot chile fields*

THE ROUTE FROM CITY OF ROCKS STATE PARK

New Mexico Route 61 north to Route 152 east
Route 152 east to I-25 south *
I-25 south to Route 187 south
Route 187 south to Route 26 south
Route 26 south to Route 27 north
Route 27 north to Route 152 west
Route 152 west to Route 61 south
Route 61 south to Home base

* ALTERNATE ROUTE

I-25 north to Route 52 north
Route 52 north to Chloride; turn around
Route 52 south to I-25 south
I-25 south to Route 187 south

From home base follow the Mimbres River to Route 152. Immediately the road narrows and starts the ascent through the **Gila National Forest,** the world's first designated wilderness in 1924. Attack the Black Range through Emory Pass at 8,228 feet and enjoy sweeping views over the Rio Grande Valley and Caballo Reservoir to the distant San Andres Mountains. For 34 miles, the road is either climbing or descending through hairpins. The thick pine forest, National Forest Service campgrounds, and scenic pullouts let you enjoy the surroundings any time you want to stop, look, and listen.

Hillsboro proper has good eats at the **Country Store and Cafe** (505-895-5306), doing business since 1879. Check out the men's room. There's enough philosophy on the walls to earn a degree in the humanities. Hillsboro, a big little town of 200 inhabitants, has an Apple Harvest Festival on Labor Day weekend which is worth planning for.

Out of Hillsboro, the narrow curves stretch out to wide sweepers, descending into lake country. At the end of Route 152 is Caballo (ka-BY-

yo, Spanish for "horse") Lake. The first exit is Route 187 south, a small road
that weaves through ranches and chile farms.

The best thing about Route 26, a straight necessary evil, is that it
intersects with Route 27. Route 27 has an equal number of cattle, cattle
guards, and curves. All three tend to spring out of nowhere. Speaking of
springs, Route 27 sometimes has running water, over the road, not under.
Heed the RUNNING WATER sign and don't mistake it for indoor plumbing.
Take cattle guards straight on, as they're slippery wet or dry. Think of Route 27 as
a warm-up for a Hillsboro appetite and Route 152's run over the Black Range.

ALTERNATE ROUTE

Extend the loop by 78 miles to **Cuchillo** (coo-CHEE-yo, Spanish for knife)
and the **Cuchillo Cafe** (505-743-2591), specializing in blue corn tortillas
and red chili. If Mom knew how to cook Mexican food, this is the way she'd
serve it up. Next door is the Cuchillo General Store. The bar, store, and game
room combine to make an Americana museum where everybody's welcome.

Looking for a place to stay and enjoy fishing? **Elephant Butte State Park**
(www.emnrd.state.nm.us/prd/elephant.htm, 505-744-5923), five miles from
Truth or Consequences and the largest lake in New Mexico, has activities every
weekend from mid-April on, including an annual **Hot Air Balloon Festival**
weekend and an annual Chili Contest. Camp on the beach or the developed
sites with ramadas overlooking the lake. Full facilities are provided.

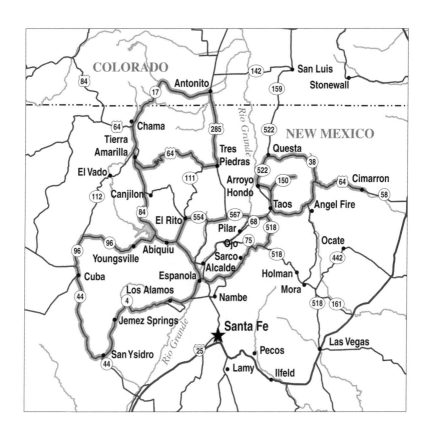

Rio Grande Valley & Santa Fe's High Pueblo Country

The Rio Grande Valley stretches from **Alamosa,** Colorado, to south of **Albuquerque,** New Mexico. Here, more than any other region in New Mexico, is the melding of cultures and history.

New Mexico's Pueblo tribes live here. Although the 19 tribes vary slightly in linguistic and tribal cultures, many of their common traditions have endured the centuries. Communal living, farming, and small herd tending are traditional ways of life. Most Pueblos welcome visitors, but please heed tribal customs. Contact each Pueblo's governor's office for specific information. See "2 x Four Corners" section for some common cultural courtesies.

The northern Pueblo Indians' community names are an example of their bond with the land.

Tesuque Pueblo . . . Te-Tsu-Geh means "cottonwood tree place."

Pojoaque Pueblo . . . P'o Suwae Geh means "place to drink water."

Nambe Pueblo . . . Nambe means "mound of earth in the corner."

San Ildefonso Pueblo . . . Po-Woh-Ge-Oweenge means "where the water cuts down through."

Santa Clara Pueblo . . . Kha P'o means "singing water."

San Juan Pueblo . . . Ohkay means "place of strong people."

Picuris Pueblo . . . Pikuri means "those who paint."

Taos Pueblo . . . Tua-Tah means "our village."

The Española Valley was first settled about 700 years ago by the Pueblo Indians. After colonizing the valley, the Spanish government moved its headquarters from Española to Santa Fe in 1609. In 1821, Mexico won its independence from Spain and New Mexico became part of Mexico until the Mexican War of 1846. New Mexico became an official United States Territory in 1851.

Georgia O'Keeffe, the famed painter and artist, chose the hills surrounding Abiquiu for her home and the object of her work. **Abiquiu Dam,** backing up the Rio Chama, creates the Abiquiu Reservoir. With campsites on the reservoir and million-dollar views, this home base choice is easy.

Trip 35 Ring Around the Rosiest Loop

Distance *213 miles*
Highlights *Beautiful curves, scenery, and history. Climbing from 5,000 feet, cresting at over 9,000 feet, down to 4,000 feet, then back home at 6,000 feet*

THE ROUTE FROM ABIQUIU RESERVOIR

Route 96 west (turns into Route 96 south) to Route 44 south

Route 44 south to Route 4 east

Route 4 east to Bandelier National Monument

Jemez Springs, New Mexico, is a jelluva place. Try the Jemez jamburger.

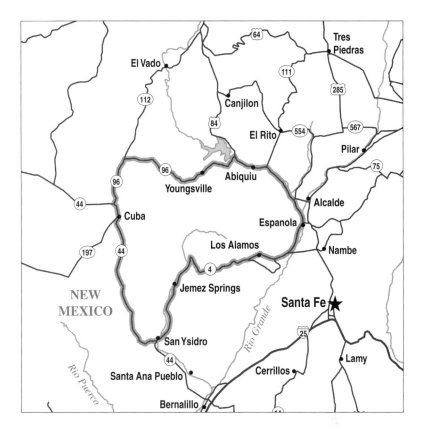

Route 4 east to Route 502 east

Route 502 east to Route 30 north

Route 30 north to Route 84 north

Route 84 north to Route 96 east

Route 96 east to home base

Route 96 is what highway taxes are for. For 53 smooth asphalt miles, lean into long sweepers, countersteer into tight S-turns, rise and descend blind hill crests, and pass through towns with names like **Coyote**. The road is sandwiched between cliffs stratified with tan, beige, white, and deep red rock, and the occasional deer, cow, or critter can dash across the front forks.

On the right, by the **Abiquiu Dam** (505-685-4561), is the 9,862-foot Cerro Pedernal. This flat top mountain, a favorite subject of artists, was so loved by Georgia O'Keeffe that she said, "If I paint it enough maybe God will give it to me." After Coyote, on the left, at 10,610 feet is San Pedro Mountain.

New Mexico still shows colorful evidence of its Spanish heritage, even if it was on the backs of others.

From **Cuba**, ride beside the Puerco River on the edge of the Colorado Plateau through the San Pedro Mountains and into the Jemez (HAY-miss) and Zia Reservations.

At **San Ysidro** the rubbernecking scenic ride is over, the road narrows, and the fun begins. Entering the Jemez Mountains, riding parallel to the Jemez River, the landscape rises on both sides 'til the walls grow into San Diego Canyon. Route 4 is a challenge. For extra mileage, take a side trip up Route 485 to the Gillman Tunnels and return.

Jemez Springs is a small community of spiritual centers. Inns, B&Bs, hot mineral baths, and my favorite, **Los Ojos Restaurant and Saloon** (505-829-3547), are all tucked in a narrow valley of ancient cottonwood trees.

After Jemez Springs, stop at **Soda Dam,** a hot spring deposit of calcium formed over the centuries from the carbonated water bubbling from the fault zone. The mineral formation created the waterfall by naturally damming the Jemez River. The dam is still growing at 300 feet long, 50 feet wide, and 50 feet deep.

Battleship Rock (www.fs.fed.us/r3/sfe/districts/jemez/picnic/battleship.htm, 505-438-7840), seen from the road, formed during one of the first lava flows in the region. Try hiking it from the picnic area at its base.

Back on the road, the coolness starts to creep into the leathers, nylons, denims, or whatever. **Valle Grande** (www.vallescaldera.gov, 505-661-3333), at 9,000 feet, is awesome. Known as the world's largest volcano, it is actually a giant caldera formed a million or more years ago from the collapse of an ancient volcano summit. Now a privately held ranch, it's not until you realize those dots on the valley floor are cows that the caldera's true size—14 miles across—becomes apparent.

After being this high it's time to come down. Follow Route 4 into **Bandelier National Monument** (www.nps.gov/band, 505-672-3861), named for **Adolph F. A. Bandelier,** a distinguished Swiss-American scholar who carried on an extensive survey of the prehistoric ruins in the region. His explorations are documented in other national monuments like El Morro. He studied the Pueblo Indians around Santa Fe between 1880 and 1886. Part of his time was spent in Frijoles Canyon, which he used as the geological stage for his ethnohistorical novel of prehistory, "The Delight Makers."

The most accessible feature of the monument is the ruins of Frijoles Canyon. You can enjoy this easy 1.5 mile walk in 45 minutes. It's a good way to cure Numbutt. Or take a two-day, 20-mile hike to the Stone Lions Shrine and Painted Cave.

From Bandelier, continue the descent to Española and then climb to home base or choose a side trip. If you have the time and energy, **Los Alamos,** famous for its glowing place in history, is home to the **Bradbury Science Museum.** If you ever wanted to go nuclear this is the place.

Trip 36 New Mexico's Rocky Mountains

Distance *222 miles*

Highlights *Two-laner heaven. Vast alpine meadows, tight mountain passes, old-time narrow gauge railroads, natural red-rock formations, raging rivers, little streams, and a living museum make this a memorable ride*

THE ROUTE FROM ABIQUIU RESERVOIR

Route 96 east to Route 84 north

Route 84 north to Route 17 east

Route 17 east to Route 285 south

Route 285 south to Route 64 west

Route 64 west to Route 84 south

Route 84 south to Route 96 west

Route 96 west to home base

If it's spring then the water is high while rolling along the Conejos River.

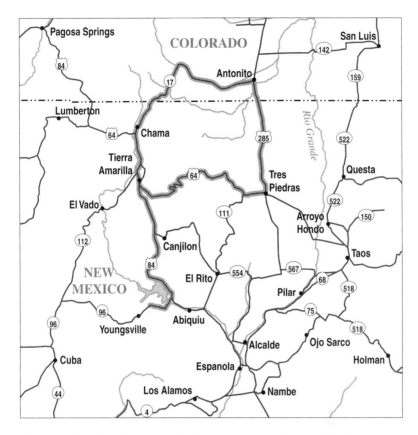

Barely getting into fifth gear, the first stop on this loop is **Ghost Ranch Living Museum** (www.newmexico.org/place/loc/favorites/page/DB-place/place/2065.html, 505-753-2155). There are a number of stories about how Ghost Ranch got its name. Many years ago the Hispanics called the area El Rancho de los Brujos—the Ranch of the Witches. Tales of wailing babies, a giant snake, a flying red cow, and a murderous brother are all part of the local legends. The Piedra Lumbre (rocks afire) Land Grant is the setting for this unique National Forest Service Museum.

If you see flying cows, pull over, but giant snakes are a real possibility. Brought to the ranch as orphans or injured, here are animals of the wild rarely seen, never mind this close.

Ghost Ranch Living Museum also encompasses **Beaver National Forest.** Less than one acre, it is the smallest National Forest in the United States. There are plenty of smaller animals, birds, snakes, and a stirring historical display of the Northern New Mexico region and its people, in word and photography.

See Mexican wolves, a very shy and elusive creature, at Ghost Ranch Living Museum. There are many rescued animals that call Ghost Ranch their home.

Next, briefly stop at **Echo Canyon Amphitheater.** Naturally carved by erosion, this theater of sandstone is a ten-minute walk from the parking spot. It is also a campground and picnic area.

After Echo Canyon, the road narrows and climbs toward alpine country. The white, snow-capped Colorado San Juan Mountains loom ahead in the distance.

Chama is the western terminus for the longest and highest narrow gauge steam railroad in the United States, the **Cumbres & Toltec Scenic Railroad** (www.cumbrestoltec.com, 888-286-2737). Built between 1880 and 1882 to serve the mines of southwestern Colorado, the railroad is now a Registered National Historic Site. It runs for 64 miles, climbing a four percent grade and cresting Cumbres (Summit) Pass at 10,015 feet. After passing through groves of aspen and pine, through the spectacular Toltec Pass of the Los Piños River, the train rumbles down into **Antonito,** Colorado, the eastern terminus.

Did I mention this Trip parallels the train most of the climb? The train leaves Chama at 10:30 a.m. If you're on the road between then and noon, there are a number of pullouts to photograph the old beast billowing black coal smoke and whistling white steam. It's worth planning.

After Cumbres Pass, continue to climb till La Manga Pass Summit at 10,230 feet and then parallel the Conejos River. If it's spring, the melt usually peaks between the last week in May and the first week in June. The river runs high and fast for even more drama. The **Conejos Canyon River Ranch** (www.conejosranch.com, 719-376-2464) sits on the river and offers rustic cabins and solitude. The cabins are fully equipped housekeeping units with one or two bedrooms plus living rooms with hide-a beds. Dinner menus are wide ranging and reasonably priced.

Road, river, and railroad end in Antonito.

Route 285 is the only portion of the trip that feels highwayish. Passing San Antonio Mountain at 10,935 feet saves you from the full super slab feeling. This 30 miles is worth the ride to get to Route 64 at **Tres Piedras.**

The next 50 miles is the quintessential alpine mountain ride. Long sweepers over emerald green meadow vistas are dashed with yellow, purple, and white wildflowers bordering mountain streams and lakes. Wild and domestic animals graze on the background carpet that shades from sweet spring-emerging yellow green to mature deep pine green. The road stays high for 25 miles. The Brazos Cliffs overlook, just before dropping dramatically off the meadow, is the place to rest the fanny and energize the mind.

A dramatic drop means 45 mph switchbacks, the fastest posted switchbacks in the Southwest. This is four miles of drop and finally levels out before connecting with Route 84 and back home.

The loop is designed to go against the traffic. There's a loss of two miles of steep climb on the east side of Combres Pass and four miles on Route 64 east for the alpine meadow backside ascent. Turn around for those spots rather than enduring exhaust.

Trip 37   High Road to Taos

Distance   *170 miles*

Highlights   *Back roads, ridge roads, and river roads with very little straight road*

The "Camino Alto" takes you through many small towns on the way to Taos. Here's one now.

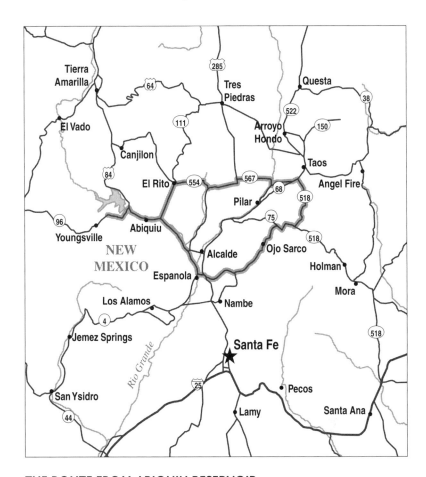

THE ROUTE FROM ABIQUIU RESERVOIR

Route 96 east to Route 84 south

Route 84 south to Route 76 east

Route 76 east to Route 75 east

Route 75 east to Route 518 north

Route 518 north to Route 68 south

Route 68 south to Route 567 west

Route 567 west to Route 285 south

Route 285 south to Route 111 north (signs for La Madera)

Route 111 north to Route 554 west/south

Route 554 west/south to Route 84 north

Route 84 north to Route 96 west

Route 96 west to home base

This loop heats up at Route 76. Called Camino Alto or "High Road to Taos," it starts out as a narrow, tree-lined back road, connecting many small towns. The High Road has a couple of low spots. If it rains there may be some asphalt streams to ford.

Chimayo, taken from the Tewa Indian word Tsimajo meaning "flaking stone" (referring to the mica in the nearby hills), was founded as a penal colony for the Spanish Empire. The Santuario de Chimayo was built over three years as the Abeyta family chapel. The church has become a legendary shrine. Hundreds of curative tales bring pilgrims at year's end to gather a pinch of healing dirt from a hole in the chapel's floor.

The ascending road climbs, S-turns, switchbacks, and meanders a ridge from here to **Truchas.**

Truchas, Spanish for trout, is built on a mesa below Truchas Peak offering a panorama of the Rio Grande Valley. Because of its isolated location, the town has continued to practice many traditional Spanish Colonial customs. Robert Redford's "The Milagro Beanfield War" was filmed here in 1986 and 1987.

Route 76 then enters the Pecos Wilderness in the Sangre de Cristo Mountains. **Trampas,** the next town on the route, is home to San Jose Church, a beautiful example of Spanish-Colonial period architecture. Route 518 starts a serious climb into Taos. These curves are delicious so gobble them up.

Route 68, the river road, follows the Rio Grande downstream. Stop along the pullouts or go past the Route 567 turnoff and watch the rafts, kayaks, and other imaginative, colorful floats pass by. This is the gorgeous Rio Grande Gorge rapids and falls. The river runs fast and deep here. It seems a different river than what ambles through southern New Mexico and barely reaches Mexico.

 JOURNEY INTERRUPTED

In the 20-mile stretch from Española to Truchas on the Camino Alto are some twenty crosses along the roadside. These are called "descansos" or reminders of interrupted journeys. Descansos comes from the Spanish verb "descansar," meaning "to rest." They are not only reminders of a journey never completed, but also a non-commercial, authentic folk art of New Mexican Hispanics.   ■

The Rio Grande runs fast and deep in these parts. Just the way kayaks and their captains like it.

The engineers who produced the specs for Route 567 must have been bikers at heart. The contractors interpreted the specs to stay exactly 20 yards from the river, resulting in a sidewinder of a road. Going upstream, this road mirrors every nook and cranny for seven miles. Plenty of free Bureau of Land Management campgrounds are for the using along this stretch.

The road crosses over the Rio Grande and climbs two miles up a fairly rough yet spectacular dirt roadbed, out the Rio Grande Gorge. Crossing the plateau, Route 111 begins the curves again. Route 554 curls up and over the Tusas Mountains, crosses the Rio Ojo Caliente, and shoots into cottonwood-lined **El Rito.**

Trip 38 Enchanted Circle

Distance *162 miles*

Highlights *Smooth two-laners through pristine forested high country, over narrow passes and deep canyons on river roads, and into ski country with or without snow, depending . . .*

THE ROUTE FROM TAOS

Route 64 east to Cimarron *

Return Route 64 west to Route 38 west

Route 38 west to Route 522 south

Route 522 south to Route 150 north

Return Route 150 south to Route 522 south

Route 522 south to Route 64 intersection

* ALTERNATE ROUTE

Connects with Trip 25 in the "Front Range" section by staying on the Santa
Fe Trail, Route 64 east

The 9,862-foot Cerro Pedernal was a favorite subject of painter Georgia O'Keeffe.

The Enchanted Circle begins and ends at **Taos**, a major spiritual and trade center in ancient times, now an art colony and gateway to major ski areas. Taos, apres-ski season, attracts tourists from all over the country. Its numerous galleries, shops, restaurants, and museums deserve browsing time. It is also home to **Taos Pueblo**, a 900-year-old settlement of the Taos Indians. **Kit Carson**, the famous mountain man and scout, lived in Taos for 25 years and died here. The Kit Carson Home, a 12-room adobe house now museum, was a wedding gift to his bride Josefa Jaramillo in 1843. A park with his grave and those of his relatives, and Kit Carson Road, Route 64, were named for him.

Heading out of Taos on Kit Carson Road (a.k.a. Route 64), you leave the bustle of tourist town behind and enter a 26-mile ride through Taos Canyon. Cresting the Palo Felchado Pass (9,107 feet), descend into the town of **Angel Fire**. No one is sure how Angel Fire received its name, but one legend has it that Kit Carson described sunlight on the frozen dew at dawn as "angel fire."

Bullet holes in the ceiling and the ghosts they created live on at St. James Hotel, Cimarron, New Mexico.

Just past the Route 64 Angel Fire turnoff, set on a hillside overlooking the tranquil Moreno Valley, is the **Disabled American Veterans (DAV) Vietnam Veterans National Memorial** (www.angelfirememorial.com, 505-377-6900). The monument rises a dramatic 50 feet, with two walls of textured surface nearly meeting at the pinnacle. Built by the family of Dr. Victor Westphall, whose son was killed in a 1968 enemy ambush in Vietnam, the memorial was dedicated as the Vietnam Veterans Peace and Brotherhood Chapel. In 1982 the DAV took full ownership and financial responsibility for the memorial. On Memorial Day, 1983, the chapel was rededicated as the National Memorial.

The road from Angel Fire to **Eagle's Nest** straightens and widens. On the left is Wheeler Peak, the geologic center of the Enchanted Circle. New Mexico's highest mountain at 13,161 feet, it dominates this mountainous region. The Sangre de Cristo Range, to which Wheeler Peak belongs, is part of the Rocky Mountains and extends into Colorado.

At Eagle's Nest, you can sit high and away from civilization. Eagle's Nest Lake's majesty comes from the solitude among the peaks at the north end of Moreno Valley.

Route 64 branches away from the Enchanted Circle. Originally part of the Santa Fe Trail, it opened in 1821 and became a major trade route between Missouri's river towns and Santa Fe. Travel over the trail ceased in 1879 but it was where Indian Agent Kit Carson, Apaches, Utes, and countless settlers once trod.

Cutting through Cimarron Canyon/Colin Nebblet Wildlife Area, Route 64 is unrelenting S-turns. The spectacular cliffs are cut by the Cimarron River through igneous rock known as a sill, which was emplaced 40 million years ago by the uplift of the southern Rocky Mountains. It's like riding a rattlesnake's back through high canyon walls of black rock. And you get to do it again. Yaba-daba-doo!

Cimarron, Spanish for wild or unbroken, was one of the legendary spots in the West's exciting history of gunslingers and range wars. Take some investigation time. The Registered National Historic **St. James Hotel** (www.stjamescimarron.com, 866-472-5019) began as a saloon built in 1873 by Henri Lambert, the personal chef to Presidents Lincoln and Grant. In 1880 the hotel was completed and immediately became a hangout for traders, mountain men, and desperadoes. Twenty-six men lost their lives there when one Clay Allison, dancing naked on the bar after having too much to drink, fired 22 bullets into the tin ceiling of what is now the dining room. The holes remain.

Other characters of the Wild West and more recent years also used the St. James as a home base. Train robber **Black Jack Ketchum** hid out there. **Buffalo Bill Cody** met with **Annie Oakley** to plan his Wild West Show. **Zane Grey** wrote "Fighting Caravans." **Lew Wallace** finished a few chapters of "Ben Hur." And **Frederick Remington** painted the nearby hills.

Finish up your day at Eske's in Taos, a local brew pub that serves tasty sandwiches, nachos, and a variety of home-brewed ales, stouts, and beers.

There is even a ghost in Room 18, as highlighted in the TV show Unsolved Mysteries. James Wright won the St. James Hotel in a poker game one night, but when he arrived to collect, he was murdered. There's a kinder ghost in room 17, believed to be Henri Lambert's first wife. Her presence is announced by a flowery perfume you can smell for 10 seconds or so. The third ghost is called the Imp. Breaking glasses, stealing toast, and general prankster stuff is his dominion.

The St. James reopened in 1985 and offers warm, friendly accommodations such as the Bat Masterson Suite, the Jesse James Room, and the Remington Room. Their menu ranges from elegant dining to homemade biscuits for breakfast. If you want to make it a weekend, the Dirty Deeds Afoot Mystery Adventures offers a western mystery where the guests play the roles of Jesse James, Annie Oakley, Wyatt Earp, or another colorful character of the Old West.

Return to the Enchanted Circle via Route 64 west to Route 38, up over Bobcat Pass at 9,820 feet, and into **Red River.** The town, high in the Sangre de Cristo Mountains, is surrounded by 20 alpine lakes, hundreds of miles of hiking trails and 60 miles of off-road trails. A large ski area, Red River is host every Memorial Day weekend to a large motorcycle rally. The town has all the services, including Carson National Forest Service campgrounds on the west end of town.

This loop offers many off-the-beaten-track diversions. One such un-beaten track is a shrine to **D.H. Lawrence,** built in 1934 on his Kiowa Ranch. It's a pilgrimage off Route 522, up a six-mile dirt road, just past the town of **San Cristobal** and one small stream. The shrine sits on a hillside with a walking path to his ashes and his wife's grave. A visitor register indicates how widely read he is. Aldous Huxley was among the frequent visitors. If you are not a fan, don't bother with the road.

The ride up to Taos Ski Valley is another winding hill climb following a creek created by snow melt, a lovely 30-mile up and down diversion. Another diversion before returning to Taos is the seven-mile ride out Route 64 west, over the **Rio Grande Gorge Bridge.** It is the second highest suspension bridge in the world (see Trip 27 in the "Front Range" section for the highest). Then back into Taos to end the loop and relax at Eske's for a brewsky (www.eskesbrewpub.com, 505-758-1517).

Eske's, a brew pub, serves delicious sandwiches and two types of corn nachos, blue and yellow. Sangre de Cristo Brewing, in the basement of Eske's, turns out fine ales, stouts, and beers. A sampler of all the beers in four-ounce servings is a bargain. The atmosphere ranges from outdoor cafe and long picnic tables to couches and sitting rooms inside. An easy place to

The Disabled American Veterans (DAV) Vietnam Veterans National Memorial, near Angel Fire, New Mexico, has a Memorial Day ride every year.

walk to, the adobe style building sits behind a parking lot, diagonal to the corner of Kit Carson Road and Paseo del Pueblo Sur (the main drag).

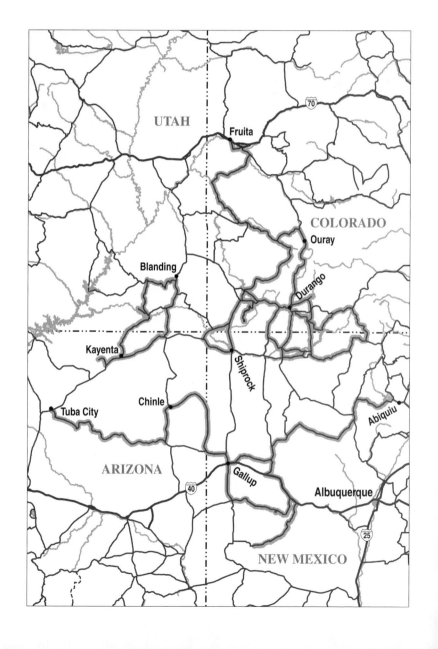

2 x Four Corners

Diversity is the key to this region, from the rocky spires of the San Juan Mountains in Colorado down to the barren desert canyons of Arizona. Natural attractions include Canyon de Chelly and the Animas and Dolores River valleys. Ancient civilizations left a mysterious legacy in Mesa Verde and Navajo Parks. It's no wonder that the Anasazi, their descendants, and other Native Americans decided to call this land home.

It is important to remember that you are visiting homelands of "The People." However translated, this is generally the name each tribal group or clan calls itself. The area is home, with all the implications of the word, and we are guests. Please respect their traditional relationship to the land. For most Native Americans, the entire earth is a living being-not just animals and plants, but rocks, rivers, and mountains. Everything contributes to the circle of life. The Navajo call this harmony "hozho."

Carved into the cliffs and valleys of the Colorado Plateau, between the San Juan Mountains and the Sonoran Desert, are the remains of an ancient civilization. The area is rich with ruins of Anasazi pueblos and cliff dwellings built more than 1,000 years ago. Like the Salado people ("Hanging on the Mogollon Rim" section), the Anasazi civilization evaporated with the water in the late 1200s. The newcomers, the Navajo and Apache, descendants of nomadic hunters and gatherers, arrived on these lands much later.

The Native Americans of the Southwest are a diverse and proud people. There are a few cultural differences between European-American and Native American cultures to respect. With some exceptions, eye contact is considered impolite. If you are speaking to a group of Navajos, some may look down or away, even though you have their full attention. You may not have a conversation at all. From childhood they are taught not to talk too much, be loud, or show off. Touching is reserved for close friends and family. The only physical contact you will see is a handshake. They consider a firm handshake overbearing and prefer a light shaking.

The land is held communally. Individual families hold traditional use rights and nearly all land on the reservation is part of someone's traditional use. Hiking or cross-country excursions without permission are trespassing. Open range is a way of communal life as well. Small herds of goats, sheep, cattle, and horses move freely along and across roads. Use caution, especially at night.

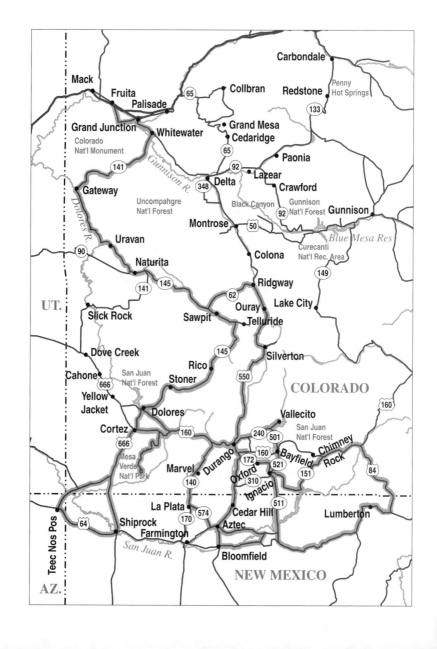

Durango Drives

Home base for these Colorado and New Mexico loops is **Durango,** Colorado. Durango offers many places to stay, eat, drink, and play. Check out the town's website for information (www.durango.com). Fellow author Toby Ballentine recommends the **Best Western Rio Grand Inn** at 400 E. 2nd Ave, 800-245-4466.

The quaint downtown of Durango, Colorado, makes a good home base for these trips.
(© 2006 Sascha Brück)

Trip 39 Four Corners Loop

Distance *272 miles*
Highlights *Mostly highway, so you can really air it out. If you have a National Park Passport Book, this loop is a two-stamper, one for Four Corners National Monument and the other for Mesa Verde National Monument.*

THE ROUTE FROM DURANGO

Take 1st Left onto E. 2nd Street
Take 1st right onto 14th Street
Left onto Route 550 south
Route 550 south to Route 160 west

Mesa Verde National Park will give you hours of delight as you climb through these fabulous ruins.

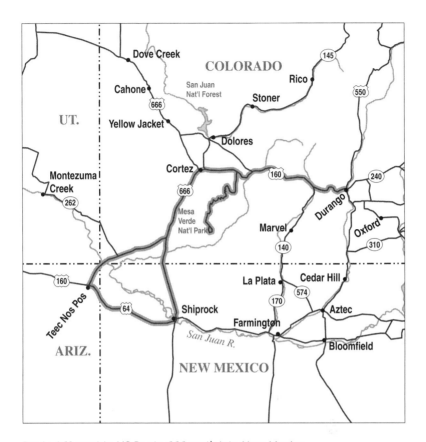

Route 160 west to US Route 666 south into New Mexico

Route 666 south to New Mexico Route 64 west

Route 64 west to Route 160 east into Colorado

Colorado Route 160 east to Mesa Verde National Park

Return Route 160 east to Durango

This loop passes **Four Corners Monument Navajo Tribal Park; Shiprock,** the town named after the sacred Navajo symbol; and **Mesa Verde National Park.** If you haven't been to an Anasazi ruins site before, Mesa Verde deserves a day by itself. The roads through the national park offer the most hairpins, sharp curves, and steep grades on the loop, all climbing high above the valley. The loop visits Mesa Verde at the end of the day, when the photography is better. The soft light will enhance the pictures of red-colored cliffs and surrounding formations.

One of the most formidable formations is Shiprock, the first stop of the

This is Four
Corners, the only
place in the U.S.
where four states
come together.

loop. Shiprock Pinnacle, a distinct volcanic plug rising 1,700 feet above the desert floor, is sacred to the Navajo who call it "Tsé bé dahi," (pronounced Sa-bit-tai-e) meaning "Rock with Wings." The Navajo hold that it was the great bird that brought them from the north.

The best picture of the formation is on Route 666/191, ten miles south of Route 64. A turnout with historical marker makes a safe dismount possible. A narrow hundred-yard path leads past the telephone wires for a clear shot. It's a 20-mile detour, but if you're a picture hound . . . woof.

Four Corners Monument Navajo Tribal Park (www.navajonation-parks.org/htm/fourcorners.htm, 928-871-6647), at 5,000 feet above sea level, is the only place in the United States where four states meet.

It's also the only place where "O.K., spread 'em" doesn't get a nervous response. It's amazing how many people place a limb in each state for that once-in-a-lifetime pose. It's a great people watching half hour with everybody's rear pointing to the sky and praying to the ancient deity, Buns.

Let-her-rip from Four Corners to Cortez. **Cortez,** which the Navajo call "Tsaya-toh" meaning "rock-water" for the nearby natural springs, is a cultural and distribution hub for the Navajos and Utes. They still come to town as in the 1800s, exchanging their hand made goods at the trading posts. Four evenings a week during the summer, Cortez has authentic Native American dances performed at the Cortez Center. Artists and artisans demonstrate their pottery and jewelry at the center, too. If you need hardware provisions, Cortez has all the big chains.

Mesa Verde National Park (www.nps.gov/meve, 970-529-4465) is one of the largest archeological preserves in the United States. Established in 1906 as a national park, the United Nations selected Mesa Verde ("green table" in Spanish) as a World Heritage Cultural Site in 1978, a designation for preserving the global heritage of mankind. As such it deserves a separate day of riding, hiking, and jungle-gym exploration, or at least a minimum of three hours. Gas up before entering, because it's 21 miles to the visitor center from Route 160.

Two six-mile loops known as Ruins Road Drive show how the community changed from the modified basket maker society of 600 A.D. to the architecturally developed Anasazi Pueblo cliff dweller society of 1200 A.D. The "Mesa Top Ruins" brochure is an excellent trail guide for Ruins Road Drive and its stop-by-stop chronology. Published by the Mesa Verde Museum Association, the booklet is available at the visitor center and at trailheads.

Hike down, crawl over, and walk through the ruins of Cliff Palace, the largest cliff dwelling in North America. The road to Wetherill Mesa is another squiggly road which follows the rim for a 24 mile round-trip, with views of the Four Corners region. There are more primitive Anasazi ruins located throughout the region available for climbing, but those in Mesa Verde National Park are the most museum-like.

Home again, home again, ancient one.

Trip 40 Roads to the Ancient Ones Loop

Distance *200 miles*
Highlights *Backroads, Anasazi ruins, dips, and curves while cruising up, on, and over high mesa terrain*

THE ROUTE FROM DURANGO

Route 160 west to Route 140 south
Route 140 south turns into New Mexico Route 170 south
Route 170 south to San Juan County 574 east (sign to Aztec)
County 574 to Route 550 south
Route 550 south to left on Ruins Road (sign to Aztec National Monument)
Return and take a soft left, across Route 550, over the bridge to Aztec
Right on Main Street. Follow to Bloomfield
Left onto Route 64 east
Route 64 east to Route 511 north

In the Four Corners area, the distances are long across desert terrain.

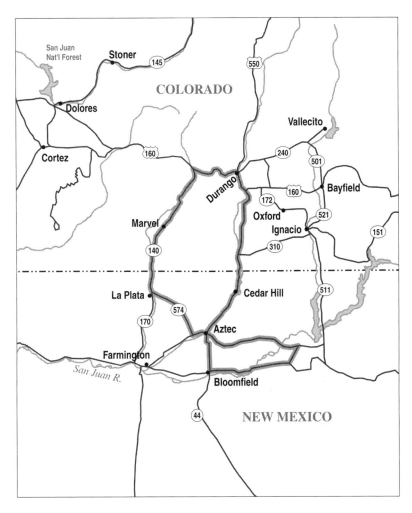

Route 511 north to Route 173 west
Route 173 west to Route 550 north into Colorado
Route 550 north to Durango

The back way into Aztec is a thin, straight asphalt trail with some bumps and heaves to keep you alert. **Aztec National Monument** (www.nps.gov/azru, 505-334-6174) is a bridge between two cultures. To the south lies Chaco Canyon, a sprawling community that flourished for 100 years between 1050 and 1150. The first dwellers at Aztec were Chacoans, or kissing cousins to them. They lived in the original pueblo for a half a century before abandoning it.

Forty to sixty years later, the pueblo was re-inhabited by the Anasazi from Mesa Verde. The Anasazi incorporated their architecture with the existing and built new structures as well. Like the Chacoans, they lived here just a few score of years before abandoning the area.

All together, these two cultures built a 450-room community centered around the Great Kiva, the Southwest's only fully restored kiva, where the residents attended community-wide events and ceremonies. Thinking the Aztecs built these dwellings, the first Anglo settlers named this site. The

Out of gas! You know how this feels after a day of hard riding.

The Great Kiva at Aztec National Monument is a spiritual ceremonial gathering place.

town took the name of the ruins. Actually, the Aztecs developed two to three centuries after the Chacoan and Mesa Verdean cultures.

At **Blanco,** the ride turns into a Mesa Mega-Curve City meets Dipsy-Doodleville. Route 511 runs between red mesa walls on the right and the San Juan River that carved them on the left. Big, bold sweepers ranging in speed from 25 to 60 mph put some frolic and rhythm into the ride. At **Archuleta,** the ride back to Aztec has more cresting hills than a prairie dog town. It's easy to get airborne, except not knowing whether the road breaks left or right means keeping the tires in contact with the hard stuff. It's tough to do this one on a full stomach.

Heading north toward **Durango,** play peekaboo with the Animas River, which starts high in the San Juan Mountains and sustains the whole agricultural area. Stay on Route 550 for downtown Durango, and a great hamburger or fajitas at the **Olde Tymer's** (970-259-2990).

Trip 41 Comic Book Cowboys & Real Indians Loop

Distance *254 miles*

Highlights *S-turns, sweepers, dips, and hairpins that pass by the antiquity of civilizations and the timelessness of fantasy and art. This is a good day for the soul.*

THE ROUTE FROM DURANGO

Durango to Route 160 east

Route 160 east to Route 172 south

Route 172 south turns into New Mexico Route 511 south

Route 511 south to Route 64 east.

Route 64 east to Route 84 north into Colorado

Route 84 north to Route 160 west

Route 160 west to Route 151 west

Route 151 west to La Plata County 521 north (sign to Bayfield)

County 521 north to County 501 north (straight across Route 160)

County 501 north to County 240 west and Durango

Chimney Rock is an astroarcheological ruin. It is a special obsevatory for a rare moonrise. You can almost hear the howl.

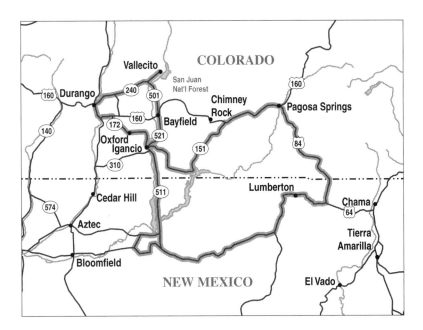

Ignacio, the tribal capital of the Southern Ute, prides itself on being a tri-ethnic town of Anglos, Hispanics, and Native Americans. A Labor Day bike rally at the Sky Ute Downs is an event to plan around. Known for their deli-cate beadwork and leather artistry, the Utes offer their wares at the Sky Ute Downs gift shop. Ignacio is also the last chance for gas for the next 50 miles.

Following the Los Piños River south to Navajo Lake, the asphalt makes sweet sweeping motions. Navajo Lake, at 6,100 feet, is a **New Mexico State Recreation Area** (www.emnrd.state.nm.us/prd/navajo.htm, 505-632-2278) complete with campground and fishing facilities. Well-known for its prize brown and rainbow trout, the lake is fed by the San Juan and Piedra Rivers. Leaving Navajo Lake behind, the loop develops into a beautiful ride along the San Juan River, then beside Manzanera Mesa, and through the Gobernador and Vaqueros Canyons. A ride for 50 miles with a speed range of 40 to 60 mph (70 mph wouldn't be pushing any limits but the police's), these sweepers offer wide vistas. Take the extra half hour for a hot run up to Navajo Lake and back down again on Route 539. Why? Because it's there! A couple of hairpins with little warning are also there.

Settle down for an afternoon ride through the Jicarilla (hic-a-REE-ya) Ranger District of the **Carson National Forest.** Wild horses, 80 in all, roam the northern third of the district, traveling in bands of five. The best time to see them is early morning or late evening. They're shy, so it's rare to see them from the road.

The Red Ryder Daisy air rifle is my weapon of choice. The museum houses the first and seven millionth one produced by Daisy Air Rifle.

From the Jicarilla District, it's on into **Dulce,** the capital of the **Jicarilla Apache Indian Reservation.** The Jicarilla Apache, primarily a hunting and gathering group, once occupied vast portions of southern Colorado and northeastern New Mexico around Abiquiu, Cimarron, and Taos. Pressure from the Comanche and European settlers eventually pushed them from their homeland. In 1887, the Jicarilla Apache were given this land as a permanent reservation.

After Dulce, climb into the **San Juan National Forest,** out the west side of **Pagosa Springs** to the **Fred Harman Art Museum** (www.harman-artmuseum.com, 970-731-5785).

According to Fred III, Fred's son, curator of the museum, and a never-ending source of stories, trying to describe **Fred Harman** is like trying to cram the Grand Canyon into a saddlebag. A cowboy who grew up and lived in the Ute and Apache hunting grounds near Pagosa Springs, he started his artistic career at the Film Ad Company of Kansas City. There Fred Harman and fellow employee Walt Disney tried their hand at a business, but failed.

In 1934, Fred created a cartoon character named "Bronc Peeler," which is what a bronco buster used to be called. Then in 1938 Bronc Peeler became Red Ryder with his sidekick, Little Beaver. The comic strip was syndicated and 45,000,000 readers of 750 newspapers on three continents followed their adventures. The first Red Ryder BB Gun hangs in the museum along with the seven millionth produced by Daisy Air Rifle. I flashed back to my youth, when I used my Red Ryder Daisy Air Rifle to shoot at neighborhood streetlights. I am old enough and far enough away to admit it now.

After the comic strip, Fred Harman turned to oils, using his photographic memory to paint detailed pictures of the Old West. After World War II, the U.S. Government used his extraordinary talent for total recall and perfect reproduction in another way. With fake documents, Fred Harman was sent behind the Iron Curtain to observe troop deployments and living conditions throughout the Eastern Bloc. When he returned, he produced 1,500 drawings detailing the things he'd seen.

Fred never had formal training as an artist and painted from memory, but you'd swear he was an expert photographer by the detail he captures in his paintings. He also authored the Red Ryder books. One on display is "Red Ryder and Adventure at Chimney Rock," our next destination.

Chimney Rock (www.chimneyrockco.org, 970-883-5359), down the Piedra Valley off Route 151, is an Anasazi cultural site and a revered place for their modern day descendants. Perched atop a high mesa at 7,600 feet, overlooking the Piedra River, the site contains ruins of an Anasazi pueblo and village. It is the highest pre-Columbian structure known to exist in the United States.

Chimney Rock is a site exciting the burgeoning field of astroarchaeology (or archeoastronomy), the study of the heavens and their impact on ancient civilizations. Chimney Rock, it turns out, is a very special observatory for a rare moonrise. The two major building phases occurred 18.6 years apart, in 1071 and 1090. The moon's orbit varies, causing it to rise from the eastern horizon at higher and lower places north and south every 18.6 years.

When the moon rises to its most northern point, it is called a "lunar standstill." At that time, the moon rises between the two spires of Chimney Rock as observed from the site of the buildings constructed. The next alignment is the year 2023.

The only way to visit the site is with a United States Forest Service guide. A modest fee supports the daily tours and special event programs. The first tour is at 9 a.m. and the last one is at 3 p.m. Allow two hours.

Chimney Rock Road (Route 151) is known locally as the Deer and Elk Highway, so be careful at dusk. The short cut to **Bayfield** is known as the Buck Highway for the same reason. They're both high mileage, sweet sweeper roads.

Trip 42 Million Dollar Highway Loop

Distance *268 miles*

Highlights *Get as high as 11,000 feet and back via 10 mph switchbacks and 15 mph hairpins over summits, 30 mph S-turns through canyons, and 40 to 60 mph sweepers through valleys. Good food and hot springs make this a tough one to do in one day.*

THE ROUTE FROM DURANGO

County 251 north to Route 550 north
Route 550 north to Route 62 west
Route 62 west to Route 145 south
Route 145 south to Route 184 south
Route 184 south to Route 160 east
Route 160 east to Durango

The million dollar view from the Million Dollar Highway of Silverton, Colorado. Is that a billion?

U.S. Highway 550 was a major road building effort that took place over decades. Until the 1940s, railroads were the only reliable means of transportation to **Silverton.** When the road reached the mountains, after World War I, the cost estimates shot up to over a million dollars—a big ticket for those days. The road to Silverton, completed in 1922, was nicknamed "The Million Dollar Highway" for the cost estimate. The last stretch to be paved, between Coal Bank Summit and Molas Pass, was in the mid-1950s.

Adding my two cents means taking the backroads around **Durango** and up deserted County Road 251, while everybody else takes the congested, straight, first 20 miles of the Million Dollar Highway. The squigglies abound on County 251, from 10-mph jogs to 25 mph S-turns to 40 mph sweepers.

The Durango & Silverton Narrow Gauge Railroad chugs through the highest mean elevation of any county in the U.S.—San Juan.

If luck is on your side, you can see the **Durango & Silverton Narrow Gauge Railroad** (www.durangotrain.com, 877-872-4607) chugging parallel to County 251 and Route 550. Cross the narrow 36-inch tracks just before joining Route 550 below **Rockwood** and enter San Juan County. It has the highest mean elevation of any county in the United States.

The ride into **San Juan National Forest** and the San Juan Mountain Range is really where the highway starts to earn its reputation. Climbing over Coal Bank Hill Summit at 10,640 feet, it snakes through Molas Pass, then drops 1,600 feet into Silverton. The vast vistas above the Animas River and Silverton are worthy of a stop and go attitude.

Silverton, at an altitude of 9,318 feet, is an old mining town gone tourist. Considering that summer temperatures range from the low 30s at night to barely 70 during the day, it's easy to understand why Silverton is the only community in the county.

The railroad first arrived from its 497-mile trip from Denver on July 11, 1882. Its path above the Animas River is even steeper than the road. If the Durango & Silverton Narrow Gauge Railroad arrives in Silverton when you do, check out the two-seater that trails the train. Its job is to put out any fires or hot cinders from the train on the way up, and to ride ahead of the train on the way back to Durango to clear rocks and debris from the line. It stops and turns around in Silverton at the 10th Street depot. I'd rather ride the two-seater any day.

From Silverton to **Ouray,** the Million Dollar Highway was originally a toll road which was well established by the 1880s. It was incorporated into the state highway system in the 1920s. Portions of the road still use the narrow gauge Silverton Railway right of ways to reach Red Mountain Pass. You can clear Red Mountain Pass at 11,008 feet, then begin a slow cliff-hanger descent to Ouray at 7,706 feet.

Ouray, "The Little Switzerland of America," boasts 150-degree, sulfur-free hot springs in a gingerbread Victorian setting. Named for the first and only Chief of the Utes, the town offers fine days and finer dining. A public **Ouray Hot Springs Pool** welcomes everybody. For a few dollars more than the public hot springs pool, enjoy the **Vapor Caves** at the **Wiesbaden Hot Springs Spa and Lodgings** (www.wiesbadenhotsprings.com, 888-846-5191), which range in temperature from 85 to 134 degrees. The Ute Indians settled here and others traveled for days to reach the waters. Native Americans still visit and perform ceremonies at the cave. The unique experience of taking a private soak in a natural hot spring used for more than 100 years can only improve your ride. Guests of the Wiesbaden can use the spa, vapor caves, and sauna at no additional charge.

Leaving Ouray is tough but then the tough get going. The next 50 miles are a spectacular ride through Pleasant Valley, seen worldwide on calendars. The Dallas Divide, at 8,970 feet, is the last hurdle into **Placerville.** From Placerville to **Telluride,** ride a high canyon road carved by the San Miguel River. Last available gas before Telluride is in **Ridgeway.**

Telluride, at the bottom of a bowl surrounded by San Juan Range peaks, is an authentic and charming Victorian ski town. The **Floradora Restaurant** (970-728-3888), offering good value sandwich fare, is but one among many. Floradora got its name from a dance troop who visited Telluride in its mining days. The **Last Dollar Saloon** is just across the street. You can bet there are many places to hang out from the Last Dollar on up.

Speaking of on up, it's time to cross Lizard Head Pass. At 10,222 feet, Lizard Head is one of the lowest passes around, so a few trucks will share the 70 mph sweepers to **Rico.**

Rico's history dates back more than 200 years. The Spaniards arrived here in 1776, followed by trappers from Taos, New Mexico. The territory was considered dangerous because of the Ute Tribe and the rugged terrain,

Rico Hot Springs hot tub. The best things in life are free.

and settlement was left to the prospectors. But in 1879, the boom was on with discoveries of silver on Blackhawk Mountain and the west slope of Telescope Mountain. The town grew to over 5,000 people. In 1893, Rico suffered the first silver panic and the population dropped to 811 in a few years.

There are still some undiscovered treasures in Rico. The **Rico Hotel and Restaurant** (www.ricohotel.com, 800-365-1971) was built in 1925 as a miner's boarding house. The restaurant offers blues and balcony dining on homemade apple, blueberry, blackberry and peach pies, and grilled chicken breast sandwiches. The menu also has a few jewels of wisdom interspersed with the offerings:

"A little inaccuracy saves a lot of explanation."

"The older I am, the less I trust the adage that age brings wisdom."

"It's a hard battle to argue with the belly since it has no ears."

"Marriage has many pains but celibacy has no pleasures."

After digesting the wisdom and meal, shoot to the next hidden treasure of Rico, the natural hot springs hot tub. Seems the townsfolk put a pipe at the end of a hot spring and let it flow into an old Jacuzzi shell. At 90 degrees and smack in the middle of nowhere, it's a great soak and free to all. Build a fire in the fire ring for a toasty dry off.

Finding the tub is easy. Coming from Telluride, cross the river and take the immediate left before entering Rico and follow your nose down the dirt road. Park the scooter in front and follow the path behind the little tin shack. It's in the middle of three ponds. Oh, one more thing, the water has a high metal content that will stain your clothes, so don't be shy!

The ride to **Dolores** eases to wide sweet sweepers, down the Dolores River Valley with the Dolores River on the left and erosion-resistant red rock walls on the right. Dolores offers the **Anasazi Heritage Center** (www.co.blm.gov/ahc, 970-882-5600) and the Galloping Goose, a composite of a Wayne bus body, Pierce Arrow touring car, and railroad undercarriage. It's near the Dolores town hall. Six "geese" were built in the early 1930s when the receivers of the ailing **Rio Grande Southern Railroad** were looking for more economical ways to transport freight and haul mail and passengers than with expensive engines.

Trip 43 Plateau to Canyons Trail

Distance *250 miles*

Highlights *Ride the bottom, middle, and top of the Uncompahgre Plateau via the San Miguel, Dolores, and Unaweep Canyons and the great canyon-making rivers of the same names.*

THE ROUTE FROM DURANGO

Route 160 west to Route 145

Route 145 north to Route 141 north

Route 141 north to Route 50 west

Route 50 west to Route 340 west

Route 340 west to Colorado National Monument's Rim Rock Drive

This trail runs through the heart of the Uncompahgre Plateau.

We're starting at the southern end and moving northwest through the plateau. If you've ridden the "Million Dollar Highway" loop, understand going north on Route 145 can be just as much fun. When I commented to the woman at the gas station in **Rico** how pretty the ride from **Dolores** to Rico was, she replied, "That's funny, the scenery really starts here." Hard to believe but it does.

Across Lizard Head Pass into **Telluride,** the riding really begins. Climbing out of Telluride along side the San Miguel River the awesome combination of time and water will amaze you. Riding halfway up the canyon walls, the road S-turns and sweeps to every contour, dumping you into **Placerville,** founded in 1877 as a placer gold mining town. Following the San Miguel through town, the canyon-hugging road snakes northwest. Crossing the river begins a steep narrow climb up and away from the rugged and remote canyon to Norwood.

Norwood sits atop Wright's Mesa with striking 360-degree views. In the 1880s, the largest ranch here was owned by Harry B. Adsit. One of Harry's cowboys was "Bud" Leroy Parker, a.k.a. **Butch Cassidy,** who rode the trail you just came from to rob the Telluride Bank in 1889.

Making a quick escape from Norwood to **Redvale,** you are surrounded by mountains, peaks, and ranges. To the southeast is the Last Dollar Range of the San Juan Mountains. Due south are the Sunshine Mountains, to the far west is Lone Cone, an extinct volcano, and to the northeast are the La Sal Mountains of Utah.

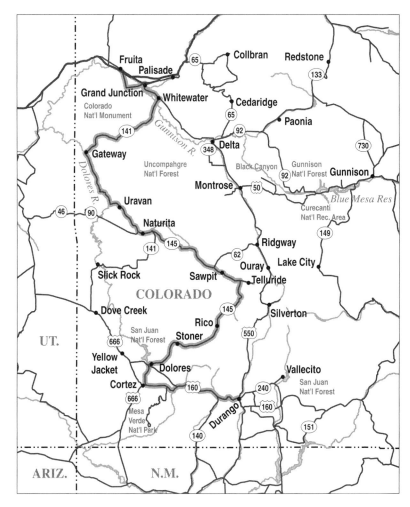

Nucla is a town with a colorful if not successful past. Home of the West's first communal experiment, it was founded by the Colorado Cooperative Company as an agricultural commune and given a name drawn from "nucleus" to indicate a socialist form of government. The experiment failed. Uravan is named for the uranium and vanadium mined here by a subsidiary of Union Carbon and Carbide Corporation. The mine tailings were used to create the first atomic bombs for the United States. Production continued until 1984, when the mine—and therefore the town—shut down. There is a $15 million project going on now to stabilize the environmental pollution left behind. If people talk about your glowing personality tonight, you'll know why.

 **ANCESTRAL ROCKIES**

The Uncompahgre Plateau is 25 to 30 miles wide and stretches nearly 100 miles north from the San Juan Mountain Range to Grand Junction. About 300 million years ago this area was uplifted into a mountain range known as the "ancestral Rocky Mountains" or "Uncompahgria." Over time the mountain range was eroded down to its roots, providing the sand, mud, and gravel to form the redrock formations of southwest Colorado.   ■

Just up the road is the Hanging Flume and a roadside turnoff. Clinging to the wall of Dolores River Canyon some 150 feet above the floor is a wooden flume. Built in 1889 and 1890, the seven-mile flume delivered 80 million gallons of water per day from the San Miguel River to the Lone Tree Placer site. Even though the site was only 40 feet above the river, technology was not advanced enough to deliver the needed pressure and volume to wash the gold from the gravel. Thank goodness for gravity.

The road now gets even tighter as you cross Roc Creek, east of Sinbad Valley, and head into the awesome slickrock formations and "redbeds" of the Dolores River Canyon. The early miners thought the sparkling salt deposits resembled the Valley of Diamonds Sinbad the Sailor encountered in the *Arabian Nights.* Roc Creek got its name from the legendary bird that carried Sinbad to the Valley of Diamonds. Well, enough of the fantasy, and now to the reality. Dolores River Canyon is a magnificent ride through steep red walls. S-Turns won't quit and you gotta hold your breath and tuck the handlebars through this extremely narrow gorge.

Four miles past **Gateway** is the Uncompahgre Fault, where the redrock meets the gray Precambrian rock of the east. Early map makers first noted a similarity between the scenery here and Yosemite National Park. The canyon changes dramatically from a broad U-shape to a narrow gorge, cutting like a hot knife through butter down these redrock formations to the granite bedrock below. The canyon is truly unique, as it is the only one with a divide in the middle causing streams to run out both ends. The Tebeguache (tab-a-watch) Utes named the canyon Unaweep, or "Canyon with two mouths," for this phenomenon. Tebeguache, by the way, is the closest Hispanic explorers could get to the Ute word Mo-Awa-Ta-Re-Wach, which means "people living on the warm side of the mountain."

After the gorge is Unaweep Seep. Residing in the nearly one-mile deep Unaweep Canyon, locally it's known as Swamp Hill. This unique wet meadow is one of the few habitats for the rare Nokomis Fritillary Butterfly. The Bureau of Land Management burns the growth off periodically to keep it a wet meadow. The normal progression of nature would be for higher brush to grow and dry the land over time.

Climbing to the Grand Valley, out the northern entrance of Unaweep Canyon, the formation is made of 1.4- to 1.7-billion-year-old rock. An overlook on the left is situated on the crest of Nine Mile Hill, a legendary wagon train route used to connect Gateway with **Whitewater.** The original 18% grade exhausted whole teams of horses pulling full loads over the hill. Now just a little exhaust and you're over.

The trail delivers you to **Colorado National Monument** and bridges to two other sections. If you want to connect with the "West Slope Slalom" section take Route 50 east at the intersection of Route 141 in Whitewater.

For a description of the home base at Colorado National Monument and Rim Rock Drive, see Trip 21 in the "West Slope Slalom" section.

Connecting to the "Grand Circle" section? Follow the trail to Colorado National Monument, grab Interstate 70 west and exit (212) at Utah Route 128. See Trip 1 for the new home base in the Canyonlands region of the Grand Circle.

Hopi and Navajoland

Home base is **Sand Island Campground** (www.blm.gov/utah/monticello/ camping.htm, 435-587-1504), three miles south of tiny but intriguing **Bluff**, Utah. The Bureau of Land Management Campground (sign says Rest Area) is a free stay by the San Juan River, the fastest flowing major river in the United States and the one used most often by colleges and universities for geological studies. There is a large petroglyph panel with five kokopelli, the hump-backed flute player of Pueblo Indian mythology, on the cliffs along the river. Jumping in the river for a cool swim after a hot day of riding clues you in on how fast the San Juan really runs. Wade in upstream from the campsites, where a small sandy beach has formed.

In Bluff, Utah's historic district, settled by the Mormons in the late 1880s, surviving homes are sheltered under old cottonwood trees. The setting still gives a sense of life in Bluff, Utah at the turn of the century. Large with wide porches, these Victorians are slowly being renovated.

Trip 44 Navajo Tribal & National Monument Loop

Distance *270 miles*

Highlights *High desert highway, with movie scenery, old ruins, natural wonders, and a great three mile climb up a cliff face*

THE ROUTE FROM SAND ISLAND CAMPGROUND

Route 191 south to Arizona Route 160 west

Route 160 west to Route 564 north (sign to Navajo National Monument)

Return Route 564 south to Route 160 east

Route 160 east to Route 163 north into Utah

Route 163 north to Route 261 north. It changes to Route 261 west later

Route 261 north to Route 316 north, turn around

Route 316 south to Route 261 west

Route 261 west to Route 95 east

Route 95 east to Route 191 south and home base

Goosenecks State Park offers a clear view of the products of water force and time. This geologic event is called an entrenched meander.

Most of the big miles in this loop should be run in early morning because it's cooler and there is less traffic. **Navajo Monument** (www.nps.gov/nava, 928-672-2700) has two unique offerings. The first is free camping from mid-May to mid-October. The second is free ranger-guided hikes to the Betatakin Ruin and Keet Seel. The hike to Betatakin ("ledge house" in Navajo) is five hours and leaves at 10 a.m. on weekends from May to September. Stay at the campground two nights and hike the day in between for an immersive experience. Betatakin was first settled around 1260 A.D. At its peak in 1286, this cliff dwelling held up to 125 people in its 135 rooms, but by about 1300, the village was abandoned.

Keet Seel ("broken pieces of pottery" in Navajo) was occupied from 950 to 1300 A.D. It has 160 rooms with six ceremonial kivas. This is a more strenuous, primitive, eight-mile, all day guided hike. It's offered from Memorial Day to Labor Day, and limited to 20 people per hike. Sign up as soon as you arrive if you don't want to be locked out.

 **ANCIENT ONES**

Anasazi is Hopi for "Ancient Ones." If you have the time and the inclination, go north four miles on Route 191 to Blanding and the Edge of the Cedars State Park (www.utah.com/stateparks/edge_of_cedars.htm, 435-678-2238), site of an Anasazi Indian ruin and a wonderful modern museum. Edge of the Cedars was established as a state historical museum in 1974. One of the largest Anasazi pottery collections in the Four Corners area is housed here. The three-dimensional sculptures of Anasazi petroglyphs gracing the outside of the building are worth the visit by themselves. This is a state facility that rivals any national effort. Not to be missed. ■

The reason there are no fees charged is these cliff dwellings are regarded as sacred by those who built them (Hopi & Zuni) as well as those who live here now (Navajo or Diné).

When returning to **Kayenta,** I would gas up before moving out to Monument Valley. If you're a western movie buff, these red sandstone buttes have been the backdrop for scores of movies over the last 50 years. A 17-mile dirt loop road is the only unescorted visitation allowed. Jeep tours with Navajo guides are available to take you to the interior of the valley.

Back on the road to **Mexican Hat,** named for the rock formation that resembles an upside down sombrero (Kahlua and milk, please). You can find the formation north of town for that all-important photo.

For the next 90 miles, we've got curves that tighten to hairpins and stretch to sweepers. They could've named the ride to **Goosenecks State Park** (www.utah.com/stateparks/goosenecks.htm, 435-678-2238) for the road, never mind the tight switchbacks of the San Juan River. At this juncture of the river see a close-up view of an entrenched meander. One of the most impressive examples in North America, the San Juan River, snakes six miles to cover 1.5 linear miles.

You won't need a goose for the next part of the ride. Just when you think you're going to crash into a sandstone mesa wall, the graded gravel **Mokee Dugway** (spelled Moki on some maps) saves the day. Built by private companies during the 1950s uranium boom, switchbacks climb the 1200 vertical feet of Cedar Mesa's cliff face in just three miles. The overlook at the top, besides providing a needed rest, gives a broad, sweeping panorama of the distant buttes of **Monument Valley** to the southwest; **Valley of the Gods,** a miniature Monument Valley, to the east; and the San Juan River below.

See the Valley of the Gods from atop Mokee Dugway.

The ride back to **Blanding** cuts across Comb Wash and Cottonwood Wash. Characterized by deep rock cuts at crests followed by steep S-turn wash bottom troughs, this roller coaster ride adds spice to a highway speed ride.

Trip 45 Canyon Canter to Gallup Trail

Distance *378 miles*

Highlights *This is a two- or three-day trail (depending on whether you explore Canyon de Chelly) of scenic beauty from canyon to high mesa through historic and prehistoric Navajo and Hopi land.*

THE ROUTE FROM GRAND CANYON

Route 64 east to Route 89 north
Route 89 north to Route 160 east
Route 160 east to Route 264 east
Route 264 east to Route 191 (old Route 666) north
Route 191 to Route 64 east (sign to Canyon de Chelly)
Route 64 east to Indian 12 south
Indian 12 south to Route 264 east

Window Rock (the formation) resides in Window Rock, the capital of the Navajo Nation.

Route 264 east to Route 666 south (US 191)

Route 666 south to Route 66 east

Route 66 east to Route 556 north (Red Rock State Park signs)

Leaving the **Grand Canyon** is a long ride along the rim. The 25 miles to **Desert View Campground** (use Desert View as a backup to Mather Campground) provide five more scenic lookouts and the Tusayan Ruin and Museum. Exiting the park picks up the Little Colorado River where the Colorado River is left behind. Be sure to stop at the Little Colorado River Gorge.

On Route 64, Route 160 around **Tuba City,** and the terrain around the Route 264 intersection, the landscape is reminiscent of the painted desert hills of the South Dakota Badlands. The road climbs and descends from mesa to mesa, village to village. Once on Route 264, feel the Hopi and Navajo historical presence.

GALLUP-ING THROUGH RED ROCK

The town of Gallup was named for the paymaster of the Atlantic and Pacific Railroad, David L. Gallup, who in 1880 established headquarters along the construction right-of-way of the southern transcontinental route. The railroad workers began "going to Gallup" to get their pay; thus the town was born and dubbed in 1881.

Home base is Red Rock State Park, six miles outside of Gallup. Red Rock has full facilities, a museum with rare Zuni Kachina dolls, and during the summer, nightly tribal dance performances at the Amphitheater. All are a casual five-minute stroll from the campsite.

For the more adventurous stroller, just behind the Outlaw Trading Post and site registration is a trail through the canyons to and around Church Rock. Stay to the left of the wash for the trail. Some hand over foot is necessary. At the top of the canyon is a 360-degree view of old adobes, hogans, and Pyramid Rock. Behind Church Rock are ceremonial fire rings. The rock is soft enough to carve.   ∎

Although completely surrounded by the Navajo reservation, the Hopi have a background and way of life different from their neighbors. For centuries, Hopi lived in pueblos villages atop or between the three mesas Route 264 travels across. The Hopi are direct descendants of the Anasazi and their way of pueblo life. Anasazi is Hopi for Ancient Ones.

Old Oraibi, sitting high on a rocky ledge of Third Mesa, is the oldest continuously inhabited village in North America. This Hopi village, with 50-mile views, has a gift shop offering the renowned Hopi crafts in pottery, coiled baskets, Kachina dolls, and silver jewelry. You can walk the streets. Please acquaint yourself with the few cultural rules in the introduction to this section and respect the people's privacy.

The next stop on Route 264 is **Kykotsmovi,** capital of the Hopi Nation and home to the Hopi Cultural Center, one of the few places to learn about the Hopi, their beliefs, and their way of life. I bought a t-shirt of Spider Woman, who introduced weaving to the Hopi and is grandmother to the North and South Poles, according to the Hopi.

Like an old asphalt river, Route 264 continues to meander through Hopi and Navajo country. Four miles east of the US 191, turn off to Canyon de Chelly (pronounced d'shay) and discover **Hubbell Trading Post Historical**

Site (www.nps.gov/hutr, 928-755-3475). The oldest continually active trading post on the Navajo Reservation, it was established by **John Lorenzo Hubbell** in 1878. It's still a crossroads of cultures where you can see demonstrations of the Navajo weaving techniques, an art which makes their rugs sought after worldwide.

Back to US 191 and up to **Canyon de Chelly National Monument** (www.nps.gov/cach, 928-674-5500). Nested on Navajo land, the monument consists of more than 100 miles of secluded sandstone canyons. The two major canyons are Canyon de Chelly and Canyon del Muerto. The area has been home to American Indians for more than 2,000 years. First, it was the temporary home for bands of prehistoric hunters. Later, the Anasazi flourished in its cliffs. There are over 100 prehistoric sites, including impressive Anasazi cliff dwellings. Now, it is home to the Navajo people. You can see their farms and hogans (six-sided huts) in the canyon much as they have been for generations.

Where the Grand Canyon is awesome in scale, Canyon de Chelly's grandeur can be experienced on a more personal level. Formed by the uplift of the Defiance Plateau and stream erosion, the canyon walls range from only a few feet at the mouth of Canyon de Chelly to 1,000 feet at Spider Rock, Tsé Na'ashjééii. The rock joins Canyon de Chelly with Canyon del Muerto.

The Canyon de Chelly has been home to American Indians for more than 2,000 years. Today, Navajo people farm the area much as they have for generations.

Church Rock, at Red Rock State Park, is an easy walk from home base.

The overlooks are divided between the north and south rims. The North Rim Drive follows the Canyon del Muerto (Canyon of the Dead), where below the rim, Anasazi pueblo ruins can be seen by the naked eye. Evidence of the Great Pueblo period is dramatically represented by the ancient "White House Ruin." It is the only place you may walk unescorted into the canyon. A two-hour, 2.5-mile switchback stroll descends 600 feet (did I say only?) to the floor. Continuity of life is evident by the Navajo farming activities on the warm, river-fed shores on the canyon floor. Cottonwoods at the bottom of Canyon de Chelly flare up into brilliant yellow-orange fall colors in mid to late October.

The climb on Indian 12 borders the Chuska Mountains' high meadows and Wheatsfield Lake. The road brings dramatic rock formations, like pickets on a fence, the entire way to **Window Rock** (www.navajonation-parks.org, 928-871-6647), capital of the Navajo Nation. The Navajo Nation is the largest Indian group in the country. Roughly one third of the Navajos live in New Mexico, the majority live in Arizona, while a few reside in southern Utah.

Signs from Route 264 lead to Window Rock Tribal Park and the geologic formation that inspired the name. Super slab from Window Rock to downtown **Gallup,** and from there onto revered Route 66 for **Red Rock State Park,** (www.ci.gallup.nm.us/rrsp, 505-722-3839), the next home base.

Trip 46   El Morro and El Malpais Loop

Distance   *257 miles*

Highlights   *Fairly uninhabited ranch and farm roads with a couple of national monuments and one inexpensive gourmet restaurant*

THE ROUTE FROM RED ROCK STATE PARK

Right out of Park onto Route 556 south

Route 556 south to Route 66 west

Route 66 west to left on 3rd Avenue, which turns into Route 602 south

Route 602 south to Route 53 east

Route 53 east to Interstate 40 east

La Ventana at El Malpais National Monument sports the largest arch in New Mexico.

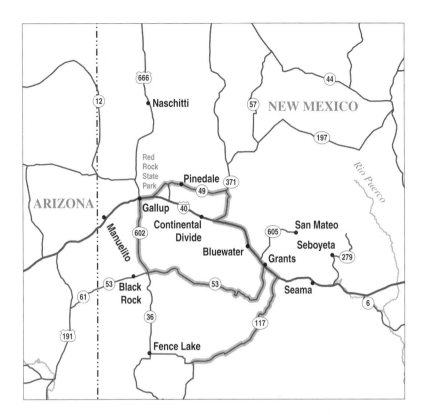

Interstate 40 east to Route 117 west

Route 117 west and return to Route 117 east

Route 117 east to Interstate 40 west

Interstate 40 west to Route 371 north at Thoreau

Route 371 north to Route 49 west (follow signs for Pinedale)

Route 49 west to Route 556 south

Right into Red Rock State Park

El Morro National Monument (www.nps.gov/elmo, 505-783-4226) is the only national monument celebrating and immortalizing graffiti. The Anasazi people called the bluff "A'ts'ina" or "place of writing on the rock." There are two pueblo ruins atop A'ts'ina. The larger of the two dates from about 1275. The pueblo measures about 200 by 300 feet and housed between 1,000 and 1,500 people in 875 interconnecting rooms surrounding an open courtyard. Their petroglyphs of human and animal figures earn the Anasazi the title of the North America's first graffiti artists.

Anasazi petroglyphs are early graffiti at El Morro National Monument.

The second wave of taggers were the Spanish. Giving the rock formation its current name, El Morro (headland or bluff in Spanish), early explorers carved their "passed by here" with the "paso por aqui" inscription. The earliest inscription carved in the soft sandstone was by the famed Don Juan de Oñate, Don Juan in 1605. Oñate became the first Spanish governor of New Mexico. The area was a constant bone of contention between the Spanish and the Pueblo Indians of the area. Eventually the Navajo, Apache, and Zuni tribes wrestled the area from Mexican control.

The third wave of scribblers were from the East. After the Mexican-American War (1846-1848), the U.S. Army made expeditions into Zuni and Navajo territory. Lt. J.H. Simpson, an Army topologist, and artist R.H. Kern dubbed the place Inscription Rock when they visited and copied the signatures on the walls. Many writers followed, some with stunning handwriting like Breckinridge or E. Pen Long's calligraphy. There's a campground at the monument and a sandstone rock in front of the visitor center for all graffitti-meisters to carve their own "paso por aqui."

The next national monument is **El Malpais** (badlands in Spanish) (www.nps.gov/elma, 505-783-4774), seated between Mount Taylor and the Zuni Mountains. Known for its 115,000-acre valley of lava flow, the landscape has been shaped by at least three flows as old as a million years.

Bandera Crater, on the western edge of the Continental Divide, is a classic cinder cone left from a much earlier eruption. Highway 117 offers an expansive scenic view from Sandstone Bluff, about ten miles down the road. At mile 14 is "La Ventana," the largest accessible natural arch in New Mexico.

Trip 47 Red Hills of Georgia O'Keeffe Trail

Distance *185 miles*
Highlights *Canyon, high mesas, and two Continental Divide crossings*

THE ROUTE FROM RED ROCK STATE PARK

Route 566 north to Route 49 east (signs to Pinedale)

Route 49 east to Route 371 north (left at T)

Route 371 north to Route 57 (Indian 9) east (signs to Cuba)

Route 57 (Indian 9) east (turns into Route 197) to Route 44 north

Route 44 north to Route 96 north

Route 96 north (changes to 96 east) to Abiquiu Dam Campground

The Floradora Restaurant at Telluride offers the chance to cool your jets on Main Street.

Route 566 is a great canyon road out of **Red Rock State Park,** an uninterrupted ride through valleys with herds of sheep, goats, and horses grazing in verdant valley meadows. Ride beside Hosta Butte at 8,620 feet. This is some beautiful empty road while everybody else takes the longer super slab route. I saw multiple pueblos, Navajo groups all across the Chaco Mesa, and just two cars traveling the 76 miles on Indian 9.

Chaco Culture National Historical Park (www.nps.gov/chcu) is one of the newest national parks in the system. This is one of the great cities of the Anasazi civilization, with more than 400 rooms. The campground fills early. Unfortunately, every entrance is at least 20 miles of bad gravel and sand roads.

Just beyond **Cuba** (are you allowed to go there with a U.S. passport?), Route 96 is what we pay taxes for. A smooth curvy road, with long sweepers and tight S-turns, cutting through the San Pedro Mountains of the **Santa Fe National Forest,** running parallel to stratified rock formations of tan, beige, white, and deep red. At the end of this route of rainbow colors is Abiquiu Dam, with campsites on the lake and million-dollar views. This is Georgia O'Keeffe Country!

See the "Enchantment Land" section for a description of Abiquiu Dam home base.

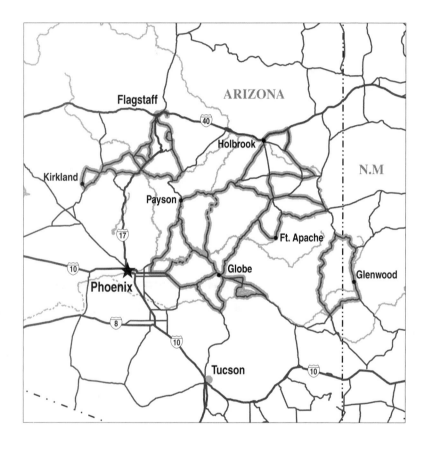

Hanging on the Mogollon Rim

The Mogollon Rim (mug-ee-YOWN) Rim, a geologic rift that marks the southern end of the Colorado Plateau, runs southeast to northwest across Arizona from the New Mexico border to just below **Flagstaff.** These nine trips, following the same direction, southeast to northwest, climb up, over, around, and down the Mogollon Rim. It's a 200-mile-long escarpment that inspired the premier writer of the western novel, **Zane Grey.** Having lived and written here, he often set his page turners here. Come explore a piece of the earth where reality inspired fiction.

Let's go hanging on the Mogollon Rim. Getting there is so much fun climbing the Mokee Dugway.

Hot Roads & Hot Springs

Home base is **Glenwood,** New Mexico. The National Forest Service maintains the seven-site **Bighorn Campground** (505-388-8201), a quarter-mile walk to town, taverns, laundry, and shower facilities.

If you're inclined to hike, San Francisco Hot Springs in the Gila National Forest is a great destination to relax. (Photo courtesy of Kim Sturmer)

Trip 48 Coronado Scenic Trail

Distance   *204 miles*

Highlights   *Ninety-four of the most sustained curvy miles in the U.S. Mountains, meadows, hairpin after hairpin, S-turn after S-turn, vistas and more. Do not be fooled by the low mileage; plan a whole day and enjoy.*

THE ROUTE FROM GLENWOOD, NEW MEXICO

New Mexico Route 180 south to Route 78 west into Arizona

Route 78 west to US Route191 north

US Route 191 north to Route 180 south

Route 180 south into New Mexico and home base

Route 180 sustains a scenic attitude with broad sweepers and a couple of S-turns, with the Mogollon Mountains to the left. Route 78 is 23 miles of

This road sign may be a warning to some but . . . definitely recommended for us!

third and fourth gear sweepers through high pasture. The last 10 miles of Route 78 drops dramatically, setting the stage for Route 666/191.

It's rare to find a road where the speed limit (10 miles per hour) is lower than the distance the speed limit governs (11 miles). This road climbs nearly 5,000 feet in 60 miles, with terrain changing from cacti of the upper Sonoran Desert to wildflower-covered alpine meadows. It's as if you were riding from Mexico to Canada in four hours.

Gas up in **Clifton** for the starting line. The next 94 miles of this journey is devoid of services. Nestled in a rugged canyon carved by the San Francisco River, the smelter town of Clifton preserved its architecture. "Copperhead," a baby-gauged steam engine, is a centerpiece display across from the restored Southern Pacific Railroad Depot.

Morenci's claim to fame is being North America's largest copper producing open-pit mine. Imagine the mountain fitting into the terrain that is now a hole. Attention rock hounds: plenty of pickings along the roadway. Just look for the familiar seashell harvesting position—head down, buns up.

On the other hand, keep your head up and tighten that helmet strap for the next 64 miles, between the eastern edge of the two million-acre **Apache Sitgreaves National Forest** and the western edge of the **Blue Range Primitive Area.** The Blue Range Wilderness area's 187,000 acres is the only remaining primitive area in the National Forest System. It remains an untouched and little known gem.

The vista broadens as this asphalt ribbon climbs, revealing peaks a hundred miles away and the valley floor 4,000 feet below. Stop at Blue Vista overlook for non-distracted sightseeing and photo opportunities of most of Southeast Arizona. It is the safest way to rest and enjoy.

From Blue Vista to the mountain highlands of **Hannagan Meadow Lodge** (www.hannaganmeadow.com, 928-339-4370) is a short hop on the edge. Built in 1924, and named after a Nevada miner turned cattle rancher, the lodge at 9,100 feet provided rest for the two-day trip along what was then a dirt road. Now guests stay in rustic log cabins, heated by fireplaces or wood stoves with "no phone, no pool, no pets." Strap on the feed bag, choosing either snack or full course varieties.

US Route 191 used to be Route 666. Don't worry, it's still a devilish ride.

Hannagan Meadow and Lodge offers rustic accommodations, as in "no phone, no pool, no pets."

In April, the snow is still piled up in six-foot embankments. It can be cool any time. May to July is peak dry lightning season, then the summer daily afternoon monsoon season begins. Start early, it isn't fun to drive a wet Coronado Trail.

From Hannagan Meadow, descend 2,000 feet to the small town of Alpine for service and civilization. Check out the **Alpine Museum** on the corner of Routes 180 and 191. Some pretty ingenious materials and old farm implements were used to make these sculptures.

Alpine is one of the best places in Arizona to see fall aspen colors. Stands of blazing gold shine magnificently against the backdrop of green pine needles. The best spot is the 9,249-foot side of Noble Mountain, near the junction of U.S. Route 191 and Route 180. Aspen leaves have undersides of white that shimmer in the wind like the gold coins Coronado searched for but never found.

Route 180 out of Alpine provides decompression time as the hairpins of U.S. Route 191 stretch to S-turns and sweepers heading home.

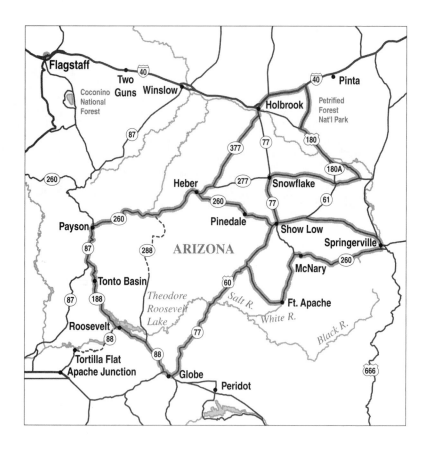

Show Low Wins

Home base for the next three trips is **Show Low**, the town named on a turn of a card. Marion Clark and famous Indian scout Croyden E. Cooley were partners and homesteaded their land in 1870, fencing some 100,000 acres. Several years afterward, Clark and Cooley, finding 100,000 acres too small, decided to break up the partnership with a poker game called seven-up, winner buying out the loser. They played all night and with the last hand Cooley needed one more point. Clark said "if you show low, you win." Cooley cut the deck and up came the unbeatable deuce of clubs. A card game is still used in town to decide the winner in a tied election.

The **Deuce of Clubs** is the street name for Route 60, the main drag, as it bisects the town. Situated on the Mogollon Rim, Show Low has plenty of choices for home base. **Fool Hollow Lake** (www.2az.us/camp-fool.html, 928-537-3680) is a state park with campsites, RV sites, fish cleaning stations, and full facilities. There are also eight remote walk-in sites.

At **La Casita** (928-537-5179), the shocks will need adjusting after this feed. Try JoAnne's special with jalapeños, melted cheese, and roasted meat on a tortilla. The combo plates come out on dishes hot from the oven.

Also try **Pat's Pizza Place** (www.patsplacepizza.com, 928-537-2337). Harley-Davidson of Phoenix has a May rally each year in Show Low. It's a natural home base.

The Apache Culture Center Museum is well worth a visit.

Trip 49 Petrified Forest-Painted Desert Loop

Distance *212 miles*

Highlights *It's like riding the Bonneville Salt Flats. Plan on three to four hours for the museum and short loops throughout the National Park. It is worth the time.*

THE ROUTE FROM SHOW LOW, NEW MEXICO

Route 77 north to right on road to Concho (sign to Concho) *

Concho Road to Route 180 west

Route 180 west to Petrified Forest National Park

Petrified Forest National Park to Interstate 40 west

I-40 west to Route 77 south

Huge trees such as this one, felled millions of years ago, have become petrified through a process by which wood cells are replaced by quartz crystals.

Route 77 south to Route 377 south

Route 377 south to Route 277 west

Route 277 west to Route 260 east

* The road to Concho is directly opposite Route 277 west in Snowflake.

Out of **Show Low,** Route 77 is smooth, with a couple of passing lanes where necessary. **Snowflake** was named after two men, Mr. Snow and Mr. Flake. I think the town has more of the flake in it. Snowflake-Taylor has a walking tour of their Pioneer homes. Together the towns have 24 historical buildings with nine on the National Register. Gas up in Snowflake, the last station until the end of the National Park 90 miles later.

The road to **Concho** is a chance to burn off the carbon deposits and air out the pipes. A few miles out of town is bupkess (nothing). You'll see the occasional 50 mph curve sign. I know everybody backs off the throttle when those pop up. Route 180 is patrolled, so brake for Smokey.

The **Petrified Forest National Park** (www.nps.gov/pefo, 928-524-6228) is really two separate parks, the Petrified Forest and the **Painted Desert.** The **Rainbow Forest Museum** at the south end of the Petrified Forest National Park is an excellent preview of what's to come. The displays inside the museum explain how petrified wood is formed and where. The dinosaurs and fossils tell the story. During the late Triassic Period, 180 to 200 million years ago, the region was a great flood plain lush with plants and animals. Volcanic activity caused these giant trees, some 200 feet in length, to fall and be washed down rivers so full of volcanic ash that the trees were buried before decomposing. The ash dissolved in the sediment, creating silica in solution, which slowly replaced the wood cells. The silica precipitated out of the solution as quartz crystals. After an unknown amount of time the wood was fully replaced by quartz, becoming petrified.

Different minerals cause the multiple colors. Iron creates yellow, orange, rust, and red. Manganese and Carbon create blue, black, and purple. The color of quartz-absent minerals is tan, white, and gray. Be sure to read the heart-rending letters of people who ripped off some petrified wood from the park and their sad burdened stories.

Behind the museum is the Giant Logs Trail. Pick up a guide and become up close and personal with the logs and processes to make them hard and colorful. There are 30 feet of still unearthed petrified wood under what you see.

The park is also home to many natural formations, historical artifacts, and desert animals. Stop at the pullouts, see petroglyphs at Newspaper Rock, and admire the Agate Bridge, where legend has it that a cowboy named Paine rode his steed across the ravine on a petrified log for ten bucks. Stroll through the Puerco Indian Ruins and take the Blue Mesa Trail, a one-mile walk down into the heart of the badlands of the Petrified Forest. The 45-minute walk through the multi-colored canyons tells the story of their formation and the continuing process of erosion.

  INSECT EATS TARANTULA

The most bizarre creature in the Petrified Forest may be the tarantula hawk, a large gun-metal blue wasp that digs a burrow two feet deep, then finding and stunning a tarantula, drags it to the burrow, lays its egg on the spider, and plugs the burrow. When the egg hatches the larval wasp has a ready-made living food supply. Yum! ■

Pat's Place in Show Low is open all night, all weekend, and it's all good.

The second park is the Painted Desert, where erosion has exposed different layers of mineral-covered earth. It is hard to believe the variety of animals that live in this barren desert of color.

The park ends on Interstate 40. Stay on the highways and straightaways till Route 260 east. If you've got to scoot home quick, stay on Route 77 south. Route 260 travels through scenic high country back to Show Low.

Trip 50   Fort Apache Loop

Distance *155 miles*

Highlights *Scenic beauty inside the White Mountain Apache Indian Reservation. The reservation ranges from 5,000 feet at the fort itself, to an alpine 9,100 feet, and encompasses almost 1.7 million acres, 240 miles of streams, and 25 lakes.*

THE ROUTE FROM SHOW LOW, NEW MEXICO

Route 60 west to Route 73 east

Route 73 east to Route 260 east

Route 260 east to Route 180 north

Route 180 north to Route 60 west

Route 60 west drops down the Mogollon Rim to **Carrizo.** It's a gentle downward-sloping two-laner. This well-paved road parallels the rim of a deep canyon for 12 miles before getting on Route 73. The road then narrows and the views extend to the horizon. Sweepers and undulating geography pass the miles. Be sure to yell "Geronimo" when you crest his namesake pass.

Next is Fort Apache and the **White Mountain Apache Cultural Center** (www.wmat.us/wmaculture.shtml, 928-338-4625). Fort Apache was established in 1870 by Colonel John Green who, in July of 1868, was ordered on his first expedition to the White Mountains and the Cibecue Apache people. He received a friendly welcome from the Apaches, who requested reservation status to protect their land and culture.

Take the small trail to the left of the museum to the edge of the cliff and see a new Apache village rising by the White River. Entrances to wickiups always face east because weather comes from the west, and everything is built clockwise from there. The village reconstructs Apache life at the time the fort was established.

A mile and a half from Fort Apache, down a rugged dirt road, are the Kinishba Ruins, marked by a small sign only visible to westbound travelers. Two stone structures, built over a hundred years ago and in ruins today, represented a massive undertaking for the Apache clan in its day. The fee to enter Fort Apache covers the entrance to the ruins.

Follow the river from Fort Apache through the town of **Whiteriver** at 5,224 feet. Beginning a 70-mile climb into the White Mountains, you're

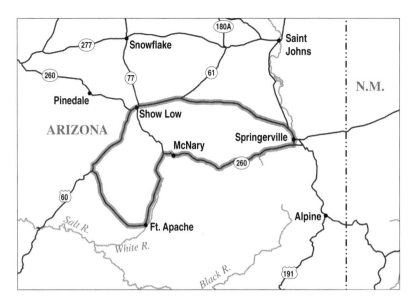

surrounded by the sweet smell of Ponderosa pines and the sight of lush meadows, high peaks, crystal lakes, and sparkling streams. Deer abound and bound, so watch out, dear!

Route 260 climbs out of Hon Dah, which in Apache means "be my guest" (not a tribute to the manufacturer). Sunrise Ski Area, peaking at 9,122 feet adjacent to Baldy Peak, is a little aside for food or drink. Take Route 373 to Greer and back if you want to extend the loop.

The Federales are out in force along Routes 73 and 260, so relax and obey all the speed limits. There are plenty of desolate, straight roads in other loops.

Choose one of two ways to return to home base. The more scenic route is back Route 260, then through the towns of **Pinetop** and **Lakeside.** Just past the towns, on the left, is the Mogollon Rim Overlook. A narrow trail runs about three-quarters of a mile from the parking lot, past 14 interpretive stops which describe the flora and fauna of the area. The trail along the rim looks down on the world's largest stand of Ponderosa pines. On a clear day, you can see the forest from the trees.

If you prefer not to drive the same roads twice, go through **Edgar** and **Springerville** to Route 60, a wide two-laner returning to Show Low in about 50 minutes. Side trips to **Casa Malpais Indian Ruins** and the **Cushman Museum of Furniture,** with displays from Renaissance to Modern, stretch the way home. Extend the loop by taking Route 73 east to catch the Mogollon Rim Overlook.

Trip 51 Scaling The Rim Loop

Distance *273 miles*
Highlights *Curves climb and descend the Mogollon Rim through canyon, forest, desert, and lake shore terrain.*

THE ROUTE FROM SHOW LOW, NEW MEXICO

Route 60 west to Route 88 west
Route 88 west to Route 188 west
Route 188 west to Route 87 north
Route 87 north to Route 260 east

Route 60 west dives through central Arizona geography. Coming off the rim is a wide, winding, sweeper after sweeper road whose dramatic scenery peaks at Salt River Canyon, a mini-Grand Canyon that lets you drive to the bottom and out the other side. Take the ride east for the curvy climb and west for the many-overlook-scenery. Oh hell, do it both ways.

The Salt River Canyon is a miniature of the Grand Canyon. The roads through it are a motorcyclist's delight, with plenty of curves and scenic overlooks.

For a description of **Globe** and Routes 88 and 188 around Roosevelt Lake, or to abort at Roosevelt Lake and the **Cholla Bay** home base, see Trip 52.

Route 260 climbs the Mogollon Rim from 3,000 feet in Star Valley to 7,700 feet in 14 miles. Then ride the edge of the rim from Forest Lake to **Show Low**. It's a level ride on the rim for the most part through tall pine forest stand. In the fall the colors explode. Generally the leaves change earlier below the rim where the Arctic air sinks, while on the rim itself, the colors change two weeks later, in mid-October. The colors in **Payson** are gone by late September.

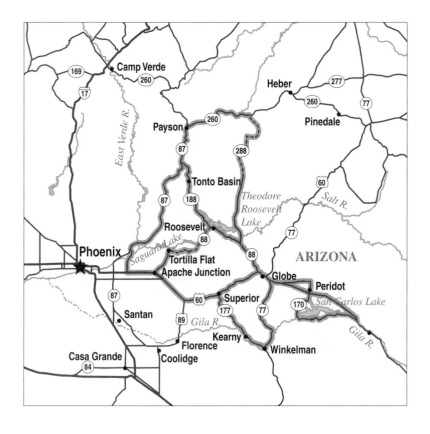

Roosevelt Lake Region

Home base for this loop is **Cholla Bay** (www.fs.fed.us/r3/tonto/recreation/ camping/tables/tbasin_tbl.htm, 928-467-3200) (choi-ya) on Roosevelt Lake. The best spot facing the water is all the way to the right. A small clump of vegetation provides some shade. There are a number of National Forest Service (NFS) campgrounds with free camping on the lake, all with pit toilets. If you like modern amenities, **Cholla Campground,** half a mile down the road from Cholla Bay, is a pay per pew.

Roosevelt Dam is the largest masonry dam in the world, built 280 feet high by Italian stone cutters and Apache laborers using granite blocks from the mountainside it spans. Across from Roosevelt Lake, only ten minutes from home base, is **Tonto National Monument** (www.nps.gov/tont, 928-467-2241). Tonto is home to the Salado Clan ruins. Named after the Salt River (Rio Salado), these people settled in shallow caves in the 1200s and remained for more than 200 years. The Salado, like their descendants, the Hohokam, were farmers. Hohokam colonists moved up the valley from Phoenix, then left the Tonto Basin between 1400 and 1450. No one knows why, but like the Mogollon and Anasazi clans, they left their homes and a mystery behind.

The 20-room lower ruins are accessible by a short half-mile self-guided tour. Make a reservation for a guided tour of the 40-room upper ruins. The guided tours are booked in advance and begin in November and end in the middle of May because of the rattlers and heat in summer. The rangers do have cancellations, so check in occasionally—I lucked out that way. This three hour, three mile hike is less steep although longer than the one through the lower ruins.

Trip 52 Apache Trail and Tortilla Flat Loop

Distance *216 miles*

Highlights *Hard curves, coupled with desert, lake, and dam vistas. Plenty of places to stop, picnic, or whatever. This is a full day of riding.*

THE ROUTE FROM CHOLLA BAY, LAKE ROOSEVELT

Route 188 north to Route 87 south

Route 87 south to Bush Highway (signs also to Saguaro Lake Recreation Area)

Bush Highway to left on Usery Pass (a four-way stop)

Usery Pass turns into Ellsworth Street

Ellsworth Street to left on Apache Trail (This is also Route 88 east)

Route 88 west (turn around at Tortilla Flat) *

Route 88 east to Route 60 east

Route 60 east to Route 88 west

Route 88 west to Route 188 north

* See Special Note about Tortilla Flat at the end of this Loop.

From the ruins of Tonto National Monument, you'll have a fine view of Roosevelt Lake.

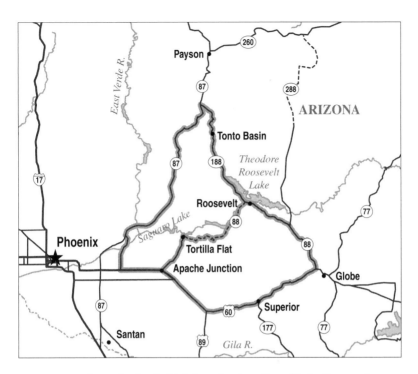

Routes 88 and 188, both of which hug the shoreline of Lake Roosevelt, are a motorcycle's oasis in a desert of straight roads and cactus. For a total of 64 miles, nothing but curves the way we like 'em, long-legged with scenery, tightening at times to second gear S-turns. The **Butcher's Hook Restaurant and Saloon** (928-479-2711) in Tonto Basin, being the only game in town, could have succumbed to the monopolistic fate of high prices and bad food. Instead the chili is 3 alarms, and the no-label ketchup bottle is homemade salsa, hotter than most. No one leaves hungry.

Jake's Corner (928-474-4675), a bar/restaurant/service station complex just before the intersection of Route 87, named for Lost Dutchman Jacob Waltz, maintains a wet sense of humor in a dry piece of earth. Stop and see the ghost town replica. Route 87 is mountainous curves on four lanes, sometimes two, but there's always a climbing lane when needed.

A quarter-mile warning and one sign are the only notice to take the left across the divided highway onto Bush Highway. The Marina at Saguaro Lake offers patio dining overlooking everything.

A four-way stop is the only clue to Usery Pass, which changes its name to Ellsworth when it enters the sprawling suburb of **Mesa**. This is a chance to purchase necessities at strip mall prices on Apache Trail, alias Route 88.

LEGEND OF THE LOST DUTCHMAN MINE

According to the Lost Dutchman legend, an opportunist named Jacob Waltz learned of gold caches hidden by the Apaches, who had no use for gold but recognized it did crazy things to the Anglos. Waltz found the hidden gold and showed up in Phoenix with enough nuggets to keep him in style for a year. Each time he ran low, off he would go to the Peralta Mine, hidden among the 125,000 acres of the Superstitions, to return with more. Records show that over eight years, from 1881 to 1889, Waltz shipped $254,000 worth of gold, not including the thousands he sold locally. The legend also has it that 60 men disappeared trying to follow Jacob on his trips to the Superstitions. The secret mine is still hidden in the mountains somewhere, despite numerous clues to its existence and whereabouts.   ■

Departing the suburban sprawl into desert again, the Goldfields Mine ghost town is the last tourist trap on the route. **Lost Dutchman Mine State Park,** at the base of the Superstition Mountains, marks the return to uncivilized terrain.

Here's our campsite at Cholla Bay. The cacophony of frogs at night is unbelievable.

All trails lead to Jake's Corner, a bar/restaurant/service station complex with a sense of humor.

Next stop on the Apache Trail ride is **Tortilla Flat** (www.tortillaflataz.com), a thriving stagecoach stop over a hundred years ago that looks like a John Wayne movie set today. The **Superstitious Saloon** (480-984-1776) offers huge half-pound burgers, killer four-alarm chili, and home-cooked Mexican food. Check out the bar and find out where the term "saddle up to the bar" comes from.

On your way back to civilization, Route 60 climbs over and through the Pinal Mountains from **Superior** to Globe. Enjoy the feel of temperatures dropping while the ride rises over these rugged mountains and canyons. This area has a legacy of mining. **Globe** and **Miami** are known as the Copper Cities. For an expanded discussion of the road from Miami to Globe, see Trip 54.

SPECIAL NOTE

If either rider or steed are skittish about dirt, turn around at Tortilla Flat. The 28-mile road to Roosevelt Lake, although graded twice a month, has some deep sand and dirt switchbacks. The all-dirt road will mean two hours to cover the 28 miles. Still, Apache and Canyon Lakes are sapphire beauties packaged in a pristine mountain desert environment. Forewarned is fore-armed and you'll need your forearms, biceps, femurs, and everything else you can muster. Have fun—I did!

Trip 53 Rimmin' Round Roosevelt

Distance *160 miles*

Highlights *This loop includes 60 miles of graded switchbacks that climb the Naeglin Rim on little-used Route 288. Ride through pristine pine on National Forest Service 512, then take a scenic descent into the Tonto Basin, rounding the lake and heading for home.*

THE ROUTE FROM CHOLLA BAY, LAKE ROOSEVELT

Route 188 south to Route 88 east

Route 88 east to Route 288 north

Route 288 north (turns into National Forest Service Road 512) to Route 260
   west

Route 260 west to Route 87 south

Route 87 south to Route 188 south

This could be bike heaven. Just south of Payson on route 87, visit with some old friends.

Don't be fooled by the low mileage. This is a full day that will test your off-asphalt skills. If there is a threat of rain, save this loop for another day. The switchbacks are graded and mostly uphill. This is a seldom viewed look at Roosevelt Lake.

Route 288 is a lightly traveled and well-maintained road. The occasional pick-up truck, signaling miles ahead via the dusty rooster tail, gives plenty of warning. Break time is 30 miles up Route 288 in the old town of **Young,** where **Antlers Saloon and Cafe** (928-462-3265) offers good eats in an authentic wood-floor saloon. Get a gander at the racks that reside in this place.

NFS 512/Route 288 continues its slope upward, a little more washboard, but nothing to worry about but dusting the steed.

Climbing down the rim on Route 260 is a joy. A wide, modern roadway hangs on, then takes the rider over the edge, plummeting 3,000 feet into Star Valley and the valley floor town of **Payson.** Payson is the best place for sundries at mall prices on this loop.

Just south of Payson on Route 87 is **All Bikes** (928-474-2526). Funny, when you see a place like this for automobiles you call it a graveyard, yet with bikes, it's like visiting bike heaven. Visit a few sets of old training wheels, and reminisce with some old friends.

Trip 54 Lake Roosevelt to Lake San Carlos Loop

Distance *260 miles*

Highlights *Mountains, open pit mines, and dams creating San Carlos Lake are on the San Carlos Indian Reservation.*

THE ROUTE FROM CHOLLA BAY, LAKE ROOSEVELT

Route 88 east to Route 60 west

Route 60 west to Route 177 toward Winkelman *

Route 177 south to Route 77 north

Route 77 north to Route 70 east

Route 70 east to Indian 6 east

Indian 6 east to Route 170 south

Route 170 south, cross US 70 to Indian 3 east

Indian 3 east to US 70 west

Route 70 west to Route 88 west

* Arizona sometimes suffers the same ethnocentric disease as California, direction by town rather than cardinal points.

By now you know the 32 miles from the Roosevelt Dam to **Globe.** It's amazing how good roads never get repetitive, just familiar. Route 60 climbs past Devil's Canyon and through rugged mining country. Descending the west side of the Pinal Mountains and dropping into Queen Valley, follow Queen Creek into **Superior.**

Stay on Route 60 past Superior to the **Boyce Thompson Arboretum** (www.pr.state.az.us/Parks/parkhtml/boyce.html, 520-689-2811). Talk about a desert bloom! Spend a couple of hours here if desert fauna and flora appeal to you.

Route 177 south starts out as bold road material, but running into the Ray Mine, a mountain turns into a molehill. The development and dominance of the mine is evidenced everywhere, from the people living in new towns built just for the personnel, to deep scarred holes in the ground, to the railroad cars carrying ore to smelter, to the smelter itself. This 32-mile ride is a course on industrial mining.

Route 77 back to Globe climbs the southern tip of the Pinal Mountains, over Pioneer Pass, then descends to the outskirts of Globe. If you're tired or not excited by another lake, head for Globe now. Turning south on Route

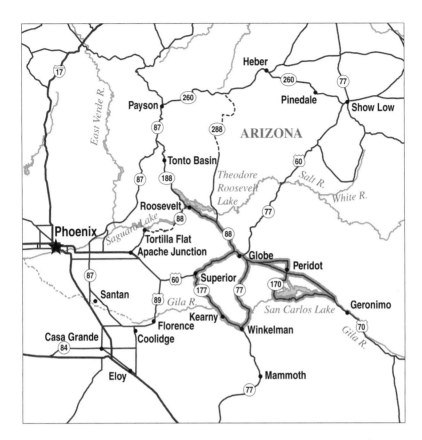

70 adds another 90 miles to the odometer as you pass through the San Carlos Indian Reservation.

Drive over **Coolidge Dam,** which backs up the San Carlos River to create San Carlos Lake. Stop at the small pullout and take a look. It is not often that people are allowed to stop on a dam this big.

The road around San Carlos Lake is narrower than most southwest roads. It also has some alligatoring. Alligatoring is when asphalt breaks up into squares before they chunk out, making the road look like the back of an alligator.

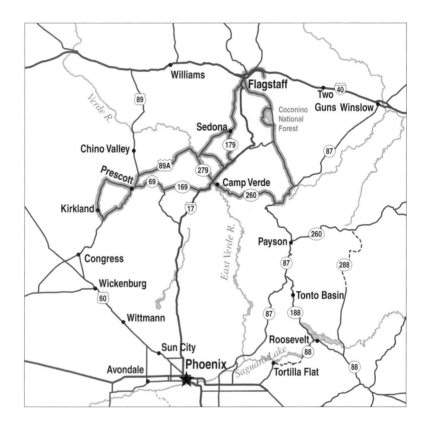

End of the Rim

Home base for these two loops is **Beaver Creek National Forest Campground** (www.fs.fed.us/r3/coconino/recreation/red_rock/beaver-creek-camp.shtml, 928-282-4119) in the **Coconino National Forest.** This small, developed (water and toilets) 16-site camp sits on Beaver Creek at a very reasonable 3,300 feet in elevation. Surrounded by 5,000- to 7,000-foot roads, this warm oasis in Verde Valley is especially appreciated in any season other than high summer. The creek produces a lullaby for your nights and a gentle wakeup call to your mornings. Use **Dead Horse Ranch State Park** as a backup campground. Just outside **Cottonwood,** it is far more developed (showers) and therefore more popular.

You can see Courthouse Butte from nearly everywhere in Sedona, and it is the site of one of the vortexes.

Trip 55 Many Towns Loop

Distance *157 miles*
Highlights *Climbing and descending through old towns, ghost towns, railroad towns, and new towns with a whole lot of curves and views*

THE ROUTE FROM BEAVER CREEK CAMPGROUND

Right out of Beaver Creek Campground to Interstate 17 south

I-17 south to Cornville Road exit

Cornville Road north to Route 89A south

Route 89A south to Old Town Loop and Clarkdale

Old Town Loop rejoins Route 89A south

Route 89A south to Route 89 south

Route 89 south to right on Whipple Street in Prescott

Whipple Street turns into Iron Springs Road which turns into Yavapai County 10

Yavapai County 10 to left on Yavapai County 15

Yavapai County 15 to Route 89 north

Route 89 north to Route 69 south

Plan to spend some time at Jerome State Park to learn more about mining.

Route 69 south to Route 169 east

Route 169 east to Interstate 17 north

I-17 north to Route 179 exit

Right at exit to home base

Cornville Road is a shortcut to **Cottonwood,** minimizing super slab exposure. Cottonwood is one of those strip mall towns that has everything a shopper desires. The Old Town Loop is a short drive through a western era Main Street complete with wood storefronts.

Continue on the loop to **Tuzigoot National Monument** (www.nps.gov/ tuzi, 928-634-5564). Tuzigoot, Apache for "crooked water," is the remnant of a Sinaguan (sin agua is Spanish for "without water") community built between 1125 and 1400. The ruin sits 120 feet above the Verde Valley. The museum gives an excellent accounting of the ruin. The ruin itself has been restored to an almost unnatural modern luster. If you have never been to a communal ruin of this period, this is a good beginning.

Stop at Jerome for a break. As recently as 1953 it was a ghost town but now it is a funky artist's colony.

The **Arizona Central Railroad's Verde River Canyon Train** (www.verde-canyonrr.com, 800-293-7245) is a 40-mile ride for railroad buffs. Leaving **Clarkdale** and following the Verde River, the train passes old mining operations, Sinagua ruins, red-rock formations, and a 600-foot tunnel. Built by 25 Swedish men in a six-month period, the rumor is 25 Swedish women were on the other side.

From Clarkdale, Route 89A climbs 2,000 feet in eight miles, up Mingus Mountain, to the liveliest ghost town in the west. Literally clinging to Cleopatra Hill, the old mining town of **Jerome** shrank from a population of 15,000 in the early 1900s to nothing in 1953 when the copper mines closed. In the late 1960s it began a revitalization as a funky artist's colony. A number of people in the town still think it's the 1960s. The entire town has been designated a National Historic Landmark. Jerome enjoys 50-mile panoramas of the San Francisco Peaks north of **Flagstaff,** the Red Rock country of **Sedona,** and the Mogollon Rim. On a Saturday or Sunday, a whole bunch of steeds are parked on Main Street.

As a tribute to its mining days, "Rawhide Jimmy" Douglas' Mansion was converted into **Jerome State Park** (www.azjerome.com, 928-637-5381). Built above the Little Daisy Mine in 1916, it was originally designed as a hotel for investors and mining officials in addition to being home for Rawhide Jimmy's family. The picnic area just above the parking lot offers a beautiful view of the Verde Valley and the rugged terrain beyond.

After Jerome, the climb continues, switchback to switchback, over Mingus Mountain and down the west side to Prescott Valley. The road straightens into **Prescott** and the Yavapai County roads slowly descend through Skull Valley (named after a large find of skeletal heads) into Kirkland Junction and Route 87 north.

Get ready because Route 87 north is a 20-mile jewel with switchbacks climbing back to Prescott. You might even want to ride it twice. The ride from Prescott to home drops from the high country back into Verde Valley. Want more curves and 30 more miles on the practice range? Reverse the directions, from Prescott back to Jerome and Cottonwood. Pressed for time? Continue on super slabs for the quickest way home.

Trip 56 Sedona Vortexes and Flagstaff Canyons Loop

Distance *210 miles*
Highlights *Curves, climbs, mountain pastures and lakes, inspiring rock formations, and ancient civilizations*

THE ROUTE FROM BEAVER CREEK CAMPGROUND

Left out of home base to Route 179 north

Route 179 north to Route 89A north *

Route 89A north to Interstate 40 east

I-40 east to Walnut Creek National Monument

Return to I-40 west * *

I-40 west to Interstate 17 south

I-17 south to Sedona/Lake Mary exit (two miles). It's Route 89A

Route 89A to left on Lake Mary Road

Lake Mary Road to right on Mormon Lake Loop Road

In search of the Sedona Vortex—are you an Inflow person or an Upflow person?

Mormon Lake Loop Road to right on Lake Mary Road

Lake Mary Road to Route 87 south

Route 87 south to Route 260 west

Route 260 west to Route 89A north

Route 89A north to Route 179 south

* See loop description of Sedona

** ALTERNATE ROUTE

Interstate 40 east to Business I-40 east (first Winslow exit)

Business I-40 east (Route 66 east) to Route 87 south

Route 179 cuts through the heart of Red Rock Country and the town of **Sedona,** an upscale place surrounded by large canyons and spectacular rock formations of deep, earthy, red brick. According to spiritual and psychic leaders, these formations create vortexes or energy centers.

The road from Sedona at 4,500 feet to **Flagstaff** at 6,900 feet follows Oak Creek through the canyon it carved. Travel on an oak-lined, covered ribbon of smooth asphalt with 28 miles of twisties, switchbacks, and red canyon walls. Along the way is **Slide Rock State Park** with its apple orchards, and Oak Creek Canyon Lookout. The Lookout presents the snake-like slither of road just conquered. The Lookout also hosts a sanctioned Native American open market. Twenty vendors along the walkway provide a dazzling display of bead, silver, and cloth artistry.

Flagstaff is a salad bowl of college students, tourists, and travelers. Vestiges of historic Route 66 (Santa Fe Road) mix motels with saloons and shopping centers. **Northern Arizona University** keeps the town young, while being the gateway to the **Grand Canyon** keeps the town churning. A place with outstanding road fare is **Mike & Rhonda's** (928-526-8138) for breakfast or anytime.

Walnut Canyon National Monument is a place to experience not just see. More than 300 rooms built into the underside of the rim line follow the canyon. The one-mile walk down, around, and through the canyon immerses the stroller in the aura of a Sinaguan community. Let out a hoot and join the ghosts of 300 Sinagua families who lived in the canyon between 1125 and 1250 A.D.

 VORTEX . . . UPFLOWS OR INFLOWS

There are two main categories of vortexes, Upflow and Inflow. In an Upflow Vortex, the energy flow is expansive. It flows upward and outward. An Upflow Vortex is best for consciousness expansion, touching oneness with the infinite, and some sensing of the future. At an Inflow Vortex, the energy pattern is inward. An Inflow Vortex is best for introspection, the resolution of old conflicts, and past-life remembrance. What makes Sedona special is the concentration of vortexes in such a small geographic area.

Bell Rock, Cathedral Rock, Airport Mesa, and Boynton Canyon are four easily accessible vortexes within the Sedona area. Even if vortexes are a little left of your consciousness, these places are beautiful to see and explore. Pick up a map of Sedona at the Chamber of Commerce and spend some time hiking and biking around. Small loops to try are Upper & Lower Red Rock Loop road, Dry Creek Road to Boynton Canyon, Mystery Mountain, and Airport Road for a view of all Sedona. ■

Not much doing at Mormon Lake. Check out the steak house walls for a bit of branding iron Americana.

The Lake Mary Road runs over high meadows and pastures by mountain lakes known for their fishing. **Mormon Lake Lodge** (928-774-0462) personifies old-fashioned high country living. Offering cabins year-round and dining with entertainment on weekends in the summer, the lodge was built in 1924 in the heyday of logging and ranching. Check out the steak house walls. Seared with authentic brands from surrounding ranches, they are a tribute to one of the wildest branding parties ever.

In the fall this loop is especially beautiful. The red and brown of oak in the Sedona area gives way to the golden aspens of the San Francisco Peaks above Flagstaff. At Flagstaff connect with the "Grand Circle" section.

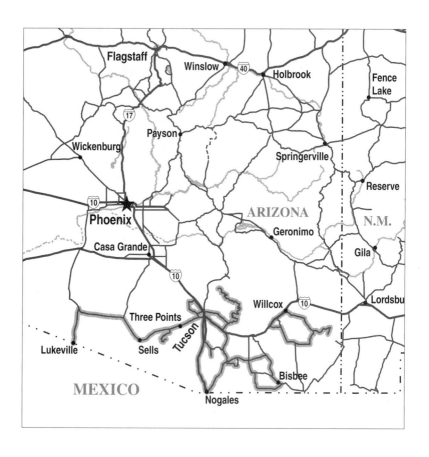

Bloomin' Desert

The extreme eastern end of the Sonoran desert dominates the landscape. The Sonoran Desert covers portions of southern Arizona and California and extends south into Mexico. Because of its low altitude and latitude, it is a warm desert relative to the other distinct deserts of North America. Only in this desert do tree-sized cacti grow. And only in the Sonoran do desert plants grow tall and densely enough in places to be called "forest." The plant life is more varied in this desert than in any other on earth. **Organ Pipe Cactus National Monument** is situated near the heart of the Sonoran Desert.

There is geologic diversity with the Santa Catalina Range to the north, Chiricahua Mountain Range bordering the east, the Huachuca Mountains to the south and many ranges in between. Traveling through multiple bioregions from the desert to snow covered mountains proves that the stereotypical desert image of Southern Arizona is a myth.

It is wide open range with miles of road accentuated with more dips and washes than curves. Dirt roads outnumber paved. The roads lead to ghost towns, old mines, wineries, tops of mountains, state and national parks, national forests, and shortcuts to every county.

Spending time in southern Arizona is like hitching up the steed and traveling back 125 years. Hundreds of things to see, experience, learn, and enjoy. The miles go to places like Tombstone, Fort Huachuca, and Cochise Stronghold, echoing stories and legends of derring-do. History, fantasy, and romantic tales of yesteryear unfold like a bloomin' desert.

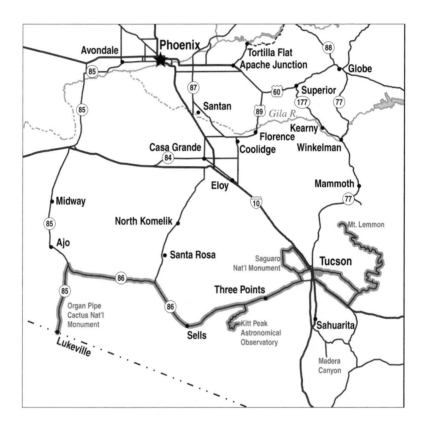

Goin' Back to Tucson

The Tucson area offers a wide variety of motorcycling pleasures in a very compact amount of miles. The choices range from unique earthly deserts to exploration of our galaxy and the universe beyond. From steep canyons to ski mountains, from ancient civilizations to modern big city treats. So rather than read let's ride . . . because we're "Goin' Back to Tucson."

The two-lane-all-weather Catalina Highway begins on the flat desert valley floor and climbs from Tucson Basin to the top of Mount Lemmon for this view (Photo © by Jeff Dean).

Trip 57 Organ Pipe to Saguaro Trail

Distance *163 miles*
Highlights *Bonneville Salt Flat-like roads run through the Sonoran Desert, with an occasional dip and a climb to a premier mountain observatory.*

These large cacti are what give Organ Pipe Cactus National Monument its name.

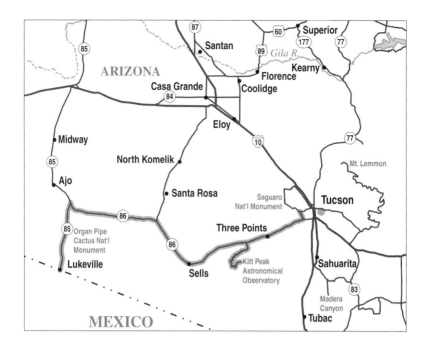

THE ROUTE FROM ORGAN PIPE CACTUS NATIONAL MONUMENT

Route 85 north to Route 86 east

Route 86 east to Route 386 south (sign to Kitt Peak Observatory) and return

Route 86 east (Ajo Highway) to left on Kinney Road

Kinney Road to McCain Loop Road to Tucson Mountain Park and home base

It's a blooming desert at **Organ Pipe Cactus National Monument** (www.nps.gov/orpi, 520-387-6849). Most of the Organ Pipe cactus found in the United States are within the Monument. Ajo Mountain Drive, within the national park, penetrates the desert with 21 miles of hard pack dirt road. Plan on two hours to complete the loop. Pick up the excellent self-paced Ajo Mountain Drive brochure at the visitor center. The 22-stop ride is the least expensive course in desert geology and plant life on earth. It will enrich the rest of your Southwest travels. The trail behind the rangers' quarters, beside the campground, identifies plants and their medicinal, tool, or food uses for the early nomadic Native American population.

Just beyond Organ Pipe Cactus National Park is **Why**. Reminiscent of the old Abbott and Costello baseball routine, no one could tell me how Why got its name. Why ask Why? Do all the provisioning, including water, there. The landscape is more moonscape through the Papago Indian Reservation.

The **National Optical Astronomy Observatories** (www.noao.edu/outreach/kpvc/contact.html, 520-318-8726) are located on Kitt Peak. Kitt Peak was selected in 1958 as a site for the national observatory after a three-year survey of 150 mountain ranges. The observatory is supported by the National Science Foundation and is the site of the world's largest collection of optical telescopes, 15 to be exact. The Mayall 4-meter telescope with a 158-inch fused quartz mirror and mounting weighs 375 tons. So delicately balanced is the telescope that the whole mechanism is driven by a one-half horsepower motor. Try balancing the scooter that well. At 6,875 feet, the 12-mile ride off the desert floor is a good way to cool down everything heated up and to break up the 130 miles from Organ Pipe Cactus National Monument to Tucson.

The National Optical Astronomy Observatory (NOAA) at Kitt Peak has the world's largest collection of optical telescopes.

The Pima Air Museum is home to the "other" crotch rockets, old and new.

Gilbert Ray Campgrounds in **Tucson Mountain Park,** six miles north of Route 86 on Kinney Road (www.pima.gov/nrpr/places/parkpgs/tucs_mtpk, 520-883-4200), is home base for the Tucson-based loops. Site C-30 is as secluded as you can get and still be near Tucson. The coyotes howl and yip, letting everybody know whose home is on this range. The best part about going to or from downtown is riding Earl's Pass Road.

While registering at the campground I asked an elderly woman waiting for the phone, "What's the best way to Tucson from here?" Scratching her head in a non-committal way, she said, "Well, just down the street is Gates Pass Road, that brings you into the center of town. Or you could go north or south to the Interstates." That was good advice. Gates Pass Road saves 15 miles and lets you ride a good mountain climber, narrow and switchbacked. Take a right onto Kinney Road, left on Gates Pass Road.

Once in **Tucson,** you'll find an endless variety of big city attractions and entertainment. The **Colorado Rockies** baseball team holds spring training here, and the **Pima Air Museum** (www.pimaair.org, 520-618-4800), **International Wildlife Museum** (www.wildlifemuseum.org, 520-629-0100), and the **Reid Park Zoo** (www.tucsonzoo.org, 520-881-4753) offer some unique alternatives.

Trip 58 Saguaro National Monument Loop

Distance *120 miles*
Highlights *Up-close desert displays its plants, animals, and strangely shaped saguaro.*

THE ROUTE FROM TUCSON MOUNTAIN PARK

Left on McCain Loop Road to right on Kinney Road
Right into Arizona-Sonoran Desert Museum. Exit left on Kinney Road
Enter Saguaro National Monument West and turn right on Bajada Loop Road
Bajada Loop Road to left on Golden Gate Road
Golden Gate Road to right into Signal Hill Picnic Area
Exit left on Golden Gate Road to right on Pictured Rock Road
Pictured Rock Road to left on Wade Road
Wade Road to right on Ina Road
Ina Road to right on 1st Avenue
1st Avenue to left on River Road

Old Tucson is where Hollywood meets the Old West.

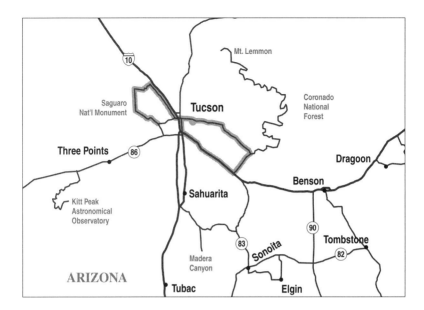

River Road to right on Craycroft Road

Craycroft Road to left on East Broadway Boulevard

East Broadway Boulevard to right on Old Spanish Trail

Old Spanish Trail to right on Freeman Road (signs to Saguaro National Monument East)

Enter Saguaro National Monument East and take left on Cactus-Forest Drive

Return on Cactus-Forest Drive to turn left on Freeman Road

Freeman Road (turns into Old Spanish Trail) and follow signs to Colossal Cave

Old Spanish Trail to right on Vail Road

Vail Road to left on Frontage Road

Exit right on Frontage Road to Interstate 10 west (sorry)

I-10 west, exit left onto Speedway Boulevard

Speedway Boulevard (turns into Gates Pass Road) right onto Kinney Road

Kinney Road to left on McCain Loop Road and home base

Saguaro Cactus (sah-war-row) National Park (www.nps.gov/sagu, 520-733-5158) is obviously named for the giant cactus. Famous for its almost human shape, the saguaro cactus begins its life no bigger than the period at the end of this sentence. What it lacks in size it makes up for in numbers. A single cactus produces over forty million seeds in its lifetime of 175 to 200 years. Only one will survive as a mature saguaro. The saguaro cactus plant is a North American original.

*They went
thattaway!*

Just before entering the westside monument (the difference between a national park and a national monument is the difference between congressional or presidential decree, respectively) is the **Arizona-Sonora Desert Museum** (www.desertmuseum.org, 520-883-2702). Rated as a top-ten museum, it houses a hummingbird aviary (wear something flowery for an up close and personal view), the Earth Sciences Complex with its cave formations, and the Riparian (stream-side) habitat where beaver and otter are viewed from an underwater gallery.

The **Saguaro National Monument** itself is divided by **Tucson**. The west side is only a few miles from home base. Take the easy hard-packed dirt Bajada Loop Drive, it's the more scenic. At the T, hang a left and enter the Signal Hill Picnic Area. At the top of the rock outcrop, an easy little trail, are pictographs drawn a millennium ago by the Hohokam people. The concentric circles and stick figure drawings have endured 1,000 years of desert harshness and still confound the experts of today. Psst, it's not listed in any literature so take a peek.

After the picnic at Signal Hill (b.y.o. water), retrace Golden Gate Road to Pictured Rocks Road east to Tucson. A few curves at speed will dust off the machine. The **Saguaro Cactus-Forest Drive** is a paved eight-mile loop. There are many hiking trails in both districts. Bring plenty of water.

Out of the monument, continue south (left) on the Old Spanish Trail to **Colossal Cave**. The ride is better than the destination, unless spelunking is a first love. Mama always taught me if you're in a hole, stop digging.

The road south to **Vail** includes a set of dips that will get the scooter airborne without trying. Just before the intersection with Interstate 10, grab Frontage Road east and rejoin Interstate 10 west for home base.

For up to the minute information on where the desert is blooming, call the Desert Botanical Gardens Wildflower 24-hour hotline at 480-481-8134.

The Hohokam pictographs at Signal Hill are examples of an early American writing system.

Trip 59   Sabino Canyon to Mt. Lemmon Loop

Distance   *85 miles*
Highlights   *Of this trip, 50 miles are a steep mountainous climb and descent overlooking the entire Tucson Basin.*

THE ROUTE FROM TUCSON MOUNTAIN PARK

Right on McCain Loop Road to right on Kinney Road

Kinney Road to left on Gates Pass Road (turns into Speedway Boulevard)

Speedway Boulevard to left on Wilmot Road

Wilmot Road to right on Tanque Verde Road

Tanque Verde Road to left on Catalina Highway (signs to Mt. Lemmon)

Catalina Highway to summit. Bear right to the ski area or left to
    Summerhaven

The Mt. Lemmon Cafe is a good spot for coffee and homemade pies.

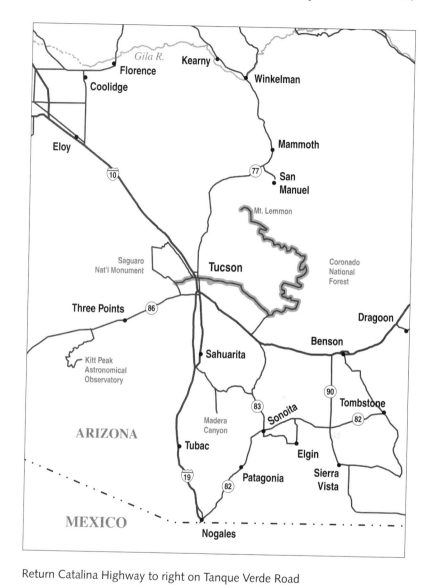

Return Catalina Highway to right on Tanque Verde Road

Tanque Verde Road to right on Sabino Canyon Road

Sabino Canyon Road to Sabino Canyon State Park

Return to Tanque Verde Road

Tanque Verde Road to left on Wilmot Road

Wilmot Road to right on Speedway Boulevard

Speedway Boulevard (turns into Gates Pass Road) to right on Kinney Road

Kinney Road to left on McCain Loop Road and home base

CLOVIS CLAN CULTURE

The human history of Sabino Canyon begins with the Clovis culture, a big-game hunting people who lived throughout southern Arizona 12,000 to 15,000 years ago. They lived off the giant Columbian mammoths, bison, and other hoofed animals of the times. About 8,000 B.C., these animals became extinct and the Cochise culture replaced the Clovis. A hunting and gathering society, the Cochise ate the successively smaller animals and plants. The Cochise were replaced by the Hohokam, farmers known for their engineered irrigation systems, who may have been descendants of the Cochise or migrated north from Mesoamerica. By the time the Europeans arrived in 1539, the Hohokam had given way to the Pimas and Papagos.   ■

Snow in Tucson! The two-lane-all-weather Catalina Highway begins on the flat desert valley floor and climbs from Tucson Basin to the top of **Mount Lemmon** (www.mt-lemmon.com, 520-749-8700). Through the **Coronado National Forest,** the Catalina Highway winds through five distinct vegetation zones.

The rock formations are a cross between the Hoodoos of Banff, Alberta, Canada, and Needles Highway near Sturgis, South Dakota. Bear left at the turnoff to the ski lift into the town of Summerhaven for **Mt. Lemmon Cafe's** (www.mt-lemmon.com/mtcafe.htm, 520-576-1234) hot coffee and homemade pies.

 CLIMATE CLIMBING

Climatologists say every 1,000 foot climb in elevation is the equivalent of driving 300 miles north. That means climbing Mount Lemmon, from Tucson's 2,600 feet to the peak at 9,157 feet, is like riding to the Canadian Border. Mount Lemmon is the southernmost ski area in the continental United States. It's quite a hoot (be sure to dress for the occasion) to go from 90-degree desert to 35-degree snowball fights in 22 miles of glorious twisting canyon-wall road.   ■

Mount Lemmon, which dominates the Santa Catalina Range, is named for **Sara Lemmon** and is the only United States peak named for a woman. She and her botanist husband spent their honeymoon in 1881 trying to climb to the top but never made it . . . on foot to the top, that is.

From the top of Mount Lemmon, scoot down the Catalina Highway to **Sabino Canyon** (www.fs.fed.us/r3/coronado/forest/recreation/camping/sites/sabino.shtml, 520-388-8300) in the **Coronado National Forest** (www.fs.fed.us/r3/coronado, 520-388-8300).

There are trails for hiking, streams and creeks for wading, and a tram for guided tours from the visitor center to upper Sabino Canyon. Get off at the top and hike down. Take a weekday, as the place gets very crowded on weekends. Check into the moonlight tours offered three times a month.

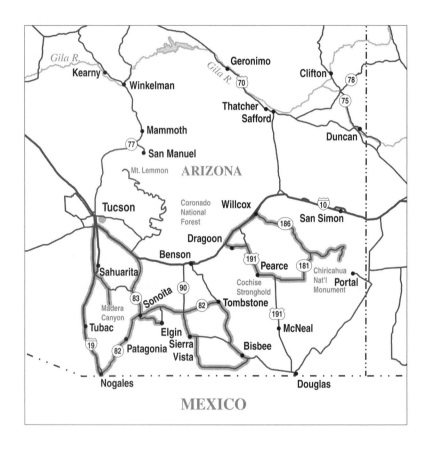

Wine and the Old West

Patagonia Lake State Park (www.azparks.gov/parks/parkhtml/patagonia
.html, 520-287-6965) is home base for the Wine and Old West country of
Arizona. The park is small, with hot showers and sites on the lake. The most
private are to the right. Watch mule deer graze by the site. If you want total
seclusion, rent a boat for a day and camp on the opposite side of the lake. Although not the most central of home bases, the setting deserves the extra
miles. Besides, the four-mile approach to the park is one of the fun roads.

From **Patagonia** it's a hop, skip, and a dip to four Old West loops. The
first loop focuses on the religious conquest of the territory. The second loop
is a one-day excursion into the commercial approach of preserving life in
the late 1800s. The third loop explores the military history of the territory.
The fourth loop samples the wine country.

For directions from Tucson to Patagonia Lake State Park, see Trip 60.

Trip 60   Missionary Position Loop

Distance *170 miles*
Highlights *From Interstate to canyon roads to dippity-doo, visit a nature lodge and the most photographed mission in the United States.*

THE ROUTE FROM PATAGONIA LAKE STATE PARK

Route 82 west to Business 89 north
Business 89 north merges with Interstate 19 north (sorry)

No wonder this rugged natural stronghold was for 15 years the home base for the famed Chiricahua Apache Chief and about 1,000 of his followers, including 250 fighting men. Large ramparts of granite domes and sheer cliffs were ready-made for lookouts.

I-19 to Tumacacori exit (signs to Tumacacori National Monument)

Return to I-19 north

I-19 north, exit at Continental Boulevard (Madera Canyon sign)

Right at exit and follow signs to Madera Canyon

Return Madera Canyon to Continental Boulevard

Continental Boulevard to right on La Cañada

La Cañada to left, at T, onto Helmet Peak Road

Helmet Peak Road to right on Mission Road

Mission Road to right on San Xavier Boulevard

San Xavier Boulevard to right on Mission Road

Mission Road to right on Valencia Road

Valencia Road to Interstate 10 east

I-10 to Route 83 south

Route 83 to Route 82 west (it feels south)

Route 82 west to home base

The first thing apparent in **Nogales,** Arizona, is the border town effect. All the merchant signs are bilingual, Spanish the larger of the two. It's a good place to stock up on necessities.

The first legitimate loop stop is **Tumacacori National Historical Park** (www.nps.gov/tuma, 520-398-2341). The conquest of the Southwest was not limited to the military. The Jesuit "blackrobes" were riding a century of expansion northward along New Spain's (Mexico) west coast when Jesuit Eusebio Kino approached the Pima settlement of Tumacacori in 1691. In 1767 King Charles III of Spain, for political reasons, abruptly banished the Jesuits from his realm. The Franciscans, who were novices in outpost missions, took over.

About 1800, the Franciscans began building a large church at Tumacacori out of the original modest Jesuit structure. Between the poverty and Mexican wars the structure rose slowly, only to be halted in 1848 by a series of Chiricahua raids. The northward expansion stopped and in fact all the missions along the San Pedro River were abandoned because of the fierce raids.

The next stop is one reason the new world was the object of conquest. Driving up **Madera Canyon** (www.fs.fed.us/r3/coronado/forest/recreation/camping/sites/madera.shtml, 520-388-8304), Continental Boulevard passes through enough climate zones for a Canadian experience. Climbing majestically out of desert basin, positioned to the north and in the middle of the Santa Rita Range, the canyon carved by Madera Creek is home to more than 100 species of birds. Ask a green-vested forest volunteer (a different type of bird) for a list of the species spotted (owl). Birding season begins in early March with the arrival of the hummingbirds and owls.

There are trails to hike. A full day hike gets to the **Smithsonian Whipple Observatory on Mount Hopkins.** For the less inclined (literally and figuratively), many trails follow the creek. Picnic spots dot the way for serene contemplation. Pick up trail maps at trailheads. The **Santa Rita Nature Lodge** (www.santaritalodge.com, 520-625-8746) and a National Forest Service campground provide overnight facilities. The lodge has cabins with kitchenettes, some with fireplaces, barbeques, and all services except food. It's a lovely way to stay high overnight. Reservations are required and make them early. Madera Canyon is a hard place to leave once entered.

Returning to the mission of this loop, the next stop is **San Xavier del Bac** (www.sanxaviermission.org, 520-294-2624). Bac, meaning "where water runs into the ground," was an early settlement named when Father Kino arrived in 1692. The mission, built by the Franciscans between 1783 and 1797, is one of the oldest American churches still in use. It's referred to as the "White Dove of the Desert" and considered one of the finest examples of mission architecture in the United States. It is arguably the most photographed mission in the United States, so be prepared for a bit of tourista.

Spend an hour or two prowling around the church and outbuildings. Climb the hill beside the church for a panorama of Tucson and the surrounding mountain ranges. The mission sits on the San Xavier Indian Reservation, which like all reservations is a federal jurisdiction. Speed limits are honored, monitored, revenue-generators.

Hang out in **Tucson,** which is 12 miles away, or scoot home via Arizona State 83, a designated scenic highway. The sweepers are a steady 2,500-foot climb to Sonoita at just under 5,000 feet. At the crossroads, take Route 82 south toward Nogales. Six miles past the town of Patagonia is home base, Patagonia Lake State Park.

Trip 61 Commercial Old West Loop

Distance *171 miles*
Highlights *Scenic highway through the Patagonia, Dragoon, and Mule mountain ranges provide 125 years of cowboy history.*

THE ROUTE FROM PATAGONIA LAKE STATE PARK

Route 82 east to Route 80 east
Route 80 east to Route 92 west
Route 92 west merges with Route 90 west
Route 90 west to Route 82 west

The highways are straight and smooth all the way to **Tombstone**, "the town too tough to die." Ed Schieffelin discovered silver near here in 1877. Because the soldiers told him the only thing he would find in the Apache-inhabited desert was his tombstone, Ed named his first claim Tombstone

High noon at the O.K. Corral—The Clanton-McLaury gang came to town to have it out.

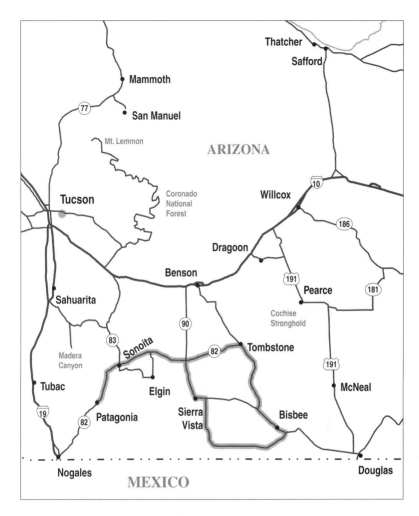

and his second The Graveyard. By 1881, there were more than 7,000 people in Tombstone, with more gambling houses, saloons, and houses of ill-repute than any other town in the Southwest. Most of the town has been restored along with the frontier action.

The town moves you back in time, with reenactments of gunfights, and buildings registered as national landmarks. The O.K. Corral attraction blends the famous shoot-out site with a diorama of Tombstone life and death. For the same entrance fee, a complimentary copy of the October 27, 1881 Tombstone Epitaph, headlining the Earp Brothers' and Doc Holliday's famed shoot-out with Ike and Bill Clanton and Frank and Tom McLaury, is included.

There they met the Earp brothers, Doc Holliday, . . . who's that? It's Marty Berke, the famous penslinger.

Also included for the same fee is the exhibition of the western photographer C. S. Fly, whose house was next to the O.K. Corral. This exhibition is worth the admission by itself. Don't forget **Boot Hill**, the original cemetery name other western towns copied. The epitaphs describe death by many causes, the most unusual being natural.

South of Tombstone, cradled in the canyons of the Mule Mountains, is **Bisbee**. At 5,300 feet, the approach from the north is through the 1/3-mile Mule Pass Tunnel. A copper mining town in 1880, Bisbee still retains a 19th-century feel and look. In the heart of old Bisbee is **Brewery Gulch and the Copper Queen Hotel** (www.copperqueen.com, 520-432-2216). Many of the rooms and all the parlors are furnished in antiques. In the saloon try a draft of Dave's Electric Beer, then wander for two hours through the hotel and Bisbee.

And this was the result of the shootout at the O.K. Corral as told by the epitaphs at the original Boot Hill.

Trip 62 Military History Loop

Distance *131 miles*
Highlights *Reminders of military efforts to settle the Southwest abound.*

Spanish missions in Arizona reflect the roots of early European settlers.

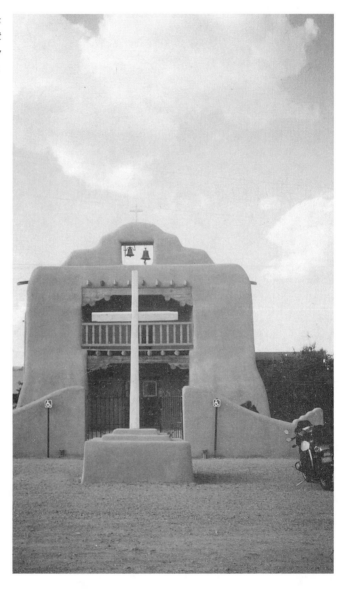

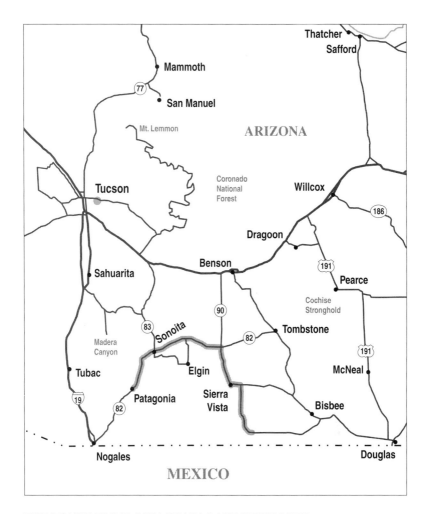

THE ROUTE FROM PATAGONIA LAKE STATE PARK

Route 82 east to Route 90 south

Route 90 east to right on Fry Boulevard (sign to Fort Huachuca Main Gate) *

Exit Fort Huachuca to Route 90 east

Route 90 east to Route 92 east

Route 92 east to right on Coronado Memorial Highway (follow sign)

Return to Route 92 west

Route 92 west to Route 90 west

Route 90 west to Route 82 west and home base

* Stop at the Visitor Center for sign-in and permission to enter. You must wear a helmet, show a valid registration, and have proof of insurance.

This loop focuses on military history and its influence on the territory. **Fort Huachuca** (huachuca-www.army.mil/sites/local) (wha-choo-ka meaning Thunder) is the oldest army fort still in operation. Established in the heart of Apacheria, at the base of the Huachuca Mountains, Camp Huachuca was founded in March of 1877. The fort's key strategic element was providing an excellent observation position of both the Santa Cruz and San Pedro Valleys to intercept the Apache's traditional escape route into Mexico, 16 miles to the south.

In 1882 the camp was upgraded to a permanent station and in 1886, hardened troopers from Fort Huachuca tracked down Geronimo and with his surrender brought to a close the Apache campaigns.

The border with Mexico became the next challenge for Fort Huachuca. Pancho Villa, after a raid on Columbus, New Mexico, became the object of the "Punitive Expedition." Led by General Pershing, it was the last major campaign carried out by horse calvary. It failed to find and defeat Villa, but the museum here captures the old west.

The **Fort Huachuca Museum** (huachuca-www.army.mil/history/museum.htm, 520-533-5736) is an outstanding custodian of southwestern military history. In the museum you can have a conversation with Colonel S.M. Whiteside, the founding officer of the fort. See a large display of Frank McCarthy's western action paintings, and read history recorded by men in service via their letters home. There is even a photo of Fiorello LaGuardia, the famed mayor of New York City, playing the coronet as a child. The uniforms, tools, weapons, and scenes of the day make drifting back to those times easy.

Just down the road from Fort Huachuca is **Coronado National Memorial** (www.nps.gov/cord, 520-366-5515), commemorating the first major exploration of the American Southwest by Europeans. The exploration was launched from Mexico City after Cabeza de Vaca and three companions, the sole survivors of a shipwreck in Florida, wandered eight years through the Southwest and brought back rumors of vast riches and golden cities.

Antonio de Mendoza, Viceroy of New Spain (Mexico), sent Fray Marcos de Niza in 1539 to confirm the rumors. Niza returned within a year with a glowing report of the fabled "Seven Cities of Cibola." Convinced by the report, Mendoza planned an official expedition and chose his friend **Francisco Vasquez de Coronado** to lead it.

The expedition, a missionary undertaking, not one of conquest, departed on February 23rd, 1540. Two years of exploration as far northeast as Kansas failed to find the Seven Cities. In utter frustration and failure Coronado led his men back to Mexico. Ten years later he died in obscurity.

 **THE APACHE WARRIOR**

The Apache warrior was one of the army's greatest foes. A nomadic tribe who took what they needed, they excelled in guerrilla warfare, ambushing, retreating, and attacking when the chance of success was greatest. The desert was a permanent ally, the Apache intimate with its ruggedness. ■

Little did he know the influence his expedition would have on the New World by introducing horses to the Native American Indians and changing their religions to incorporate some of the priests' teachings. Coronado also brought back knowledge allowing further expeditions which helped to create the unique Hispanic-American culture of today.

Trip 63 Hedonist Loop

Distance *50 miles*
Highlights *. . . and a good thing, too*

THE ROUTE FROM PATAGONIA LAKE STATE PARK

Route 82 east to Route 83 south

Route 83 south to left on Elgin Road (sign to Elgin)

Bear right after Karen's Cafe to Canelo Road (signs to Sonoita Vineyards)

Return to Karen's Cafe

Walk next door to Santa Cruz Winery

Walk back to Karen's for lunch

Walk behind Karen's to the Chapel

Return to Karen's

Return on Elgin Road to Route 83

Route 83 north to Route 82 west

Route 82 west to home base

Sonoita Vineyards are a desert bouquet.

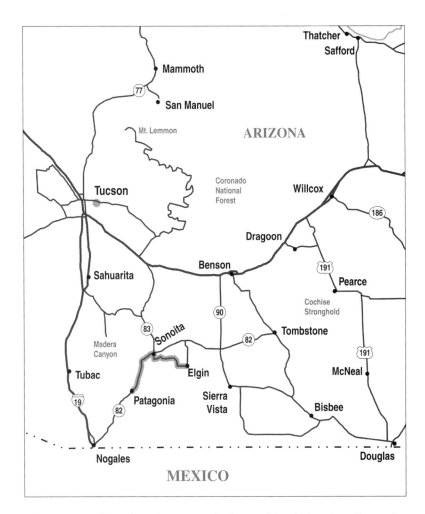

I hesitate to call it a loop but given all the good hard historic miles you've put on, this one is for pleasure of a different sort, therefore not many miles and plenty of time to sample the fares and wares.

Park at **Karen's Wine Country Cafe** (520-455-5282) in **Elgin,** make reservations, then depending on your energies you can walk the three miles or ride on washboard Canelo Road to **Sonoita Vineyards** (www.sonoita-vineyards.com, 520-455-5893). The wines are excellent. The reds are bold, even the young ones.

Karen's itself was originally the 90-year-old **Elgin General Store and Post Office.** With reservations (for walk-ins are almost non-existent), sit inside or out, surrounded by cottonwoods and the beautiful Mustang Mountains for a backdrop. The unique flavor combinations with the ultra-fresh foods will make you wish you could spend the next week just sampling the offerings. For lunch, I had a sweet pepper, mushroom, and leek soup for starters, and a vermicelli with sweet peppers, onions, pine nuts, garlic, and Italian sausage for a main dish. All desserts are homemade. The Callaghan in Callaghan wines is Karen.

Next door to Karen's is the **Santa Cruz Winery** (520-455-5373). The remarkable distinction of this producer of dry wines is that the wines are kosher. Having stereotyped kosher wines as sweet as sugar, I was quickly and pleasantly able to discard the stereotype. Where was the Santa Cruz Winery when I was weaned on Manischewitz?

"Stick 'em up!"

Even kosher wine is dry in the desert.

Just behind Karen's is La Capilla de Santa Marie Consoladora de Los Afligidos, Chapel of the Blessed Mother Consoler of the Afflicted, a non-denominational chapel with a simplicity, except for the name, anyone can enjoy. Check out the window dressings.

If you haven't had your fill by now, back in Sonoita is **Er Pastaro** (520-455-5821), an Italian restaurant serving only pasta dishes. Being the only main course offerings, you know it has to be very good. Famous people from all over the world dine in the casual elegance. As a testimony to its fame the walls of Er Pastaro are plastered with pictures of celebrities who have partaken of its culinary concoctions.

Trip 64 On the Trail of Chiricahua Apache Hideouts Loop

Distance *145 miles*

Highlights *Scenic drives from mountain ranges to mountain trails lead to a "Wonderland of Rocks" and Cochise's Stronghold.*

THE ROUTE FROM CHIRICAHUA NATIONAL MONUMENT

Exit left from Chiricahua National Monument to Route 181 west

Route 181 west to Route 666 (Route 191) north

Route 666/191 north to left on Cochise Stronghold Road

Return to Route 666/191 north to left on Dragoon Road

Dragoon Road to right into Amerind Foundation Museum

Return to Dragoon Road, turn right to Interstate 10 east

I-10 east to Wilcox (Route 186 south)

Route 186 south to entrance of Chiricahua National Monument

Even today, Cochise's stronghold can be daunting.

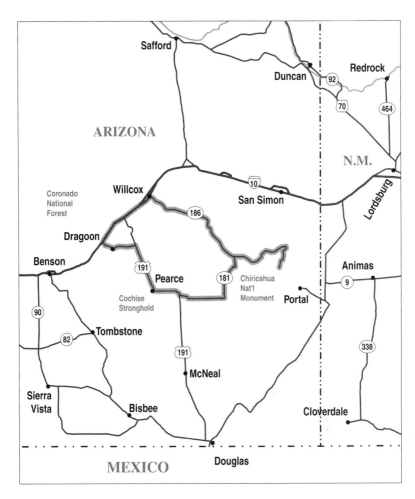

Home base is hiding out in **Chiricahua National Monument** (www.nps.gov/chir, 520-824-3560 ext. 302), ancestral homeland of the Chiricahua Apaches, who lived in the southeast corner of Arizona between the Dragoon Mountains and their namesake Chiricahua Mountains. Because of their proximity to Mexico and remoteness of the territory, the Chiricahua Apaches were the last of the six tribes in the Apache Nation to be controlled.

Among the first pioneers to settle in the area were Neil and Emma Erickson, a Swedish immigrant couple. Their daughter Lillian and her husband Ed Riggs petitioned for national park status to protect the wondrous rock formations and wilderness. Two years later, in 1924, the Chiricahua National Monument was established.

OF COCHISE & GERONIMO

The Chiricahua Apaches were one of the few clans to have a hereditary chief, Cochise. Cochise believed the white man and Chiricahua Apaches could live in peace with much to teach each other. Settlers streamed through Apache Pass into the Arizona Territory unmolested. In 1858 Cochise allowed the building of a Butterfield Stage stop.

Then in 1861 a blunder by an inexperienced U.S. Army Lieutenant named Bascom destroyed the peace. Bascom wrongly accused Cochise of stealing cattle and kidnapping a boy from his ranch home. The Army captured Cochise, one of his brothers, and two nephews. Cochise escaped and took hostages of his own, hoping to make an exchange and save his kinfolk. The Army hung the captured Apaches, so Cochise retaliated by killing the hostages he held. For the next 11 years, thousands were killed and settlements destroyed.

Cochise, a master strategist and leader, was never conquered in battle. In 1872 he came to terms with the white man and lived his remaining two years in peace. Upon his death, he was secretly buried somewhere in his stronghold. The Apaches are not allowed to speak of the dead, so the exact location of his grave is still a mystery today.

As the continuous encroachment of broken treaties and promises enclosed the clan, the Chiricahua Apaches split into factions. The reservation was closed and moved to the San Carlos Reservation (see Trip 54 in the section "Hanging on the Rim"), totally abandoning the rights of the Chiricahua Apaches to live on their own land.

In 1876, Geronimo, Chief of the Chiricahua Apaches, and his clan jumped the reservation and launched attacks on settlers. The armies of the United States and Mexico couldn't find them. Geronimo and his band, concerned for their women and children, tired of being hunted and hounded, surrendered in 1886.   ∎

Exploring Chiricahua National Monument is exploring a fantasy world of extraordinary rock sculptures. The Chiricahua Apaches called it "Land of the Standing-up Rocks." Later termed the "Wonderland of Rocks" by the pioneers, this is a forest of spires, columns, and mammoth balanced rocks weighing hundreds of tons sitting on tiny pedestals. Explore by road, trail, or both.

There is a scenic six-mile drive to Massai Point and an off-shoot to Sugarloaf Mountain. There are more than 20 miles of hiking trails. Pick up a free map and the companion "Hiking in Chiricahua National Monument" (ten cents) to help you determine degree of difficulty, distance, and approximate hiking times. The trails are superbly maintained. The Echo Canyon Trail, ranging from 6,000 to 7,000 feet, is more like hiking the Sierra Madres of Mexico than any highlands of the United States. This "sky island," surrounded by the Chihuahua and Sonoran deserts, has vegetation and wildlife that migrated north from Mexico. An abundance of rare birds like the sulfur-bellied flycatcher, Mexican chickadees, and coppery-tailed trogons live with mammals like the Apache fox squirrel and coatimundis (a raccoon-like animal with a prehensile tail). Douglas fir, aspen, and Ponderosa pine cover the highest slopes.

If doing one hike, the Heart of Rocks Trail is it, trust me. If you're planning to stay longer, the campground is surrounded by spires and immersed in a forest. A magnificent place to be.

Across the Sulphur Springs Valley from Chiricahua National Monument is **Cochise Stronghold Canyon** (www.fs.fed.us/r3/coronado/forest/recreation/camping/sites/cochise_stronghold.shtml, 520-388-8300). Lying in the heart of the Dragoon Mountains, Cochise Stronghold Road (sign on Route 191) is ten miles of washboard, fording three streams (careful—if it has just rained they become rivers). No wonder this rugged natural stronghold was for 15 years the home base for the famed Chiricahua Apache Chief and about 1,000 of his followers, including 250 fighting men. Large ramparts of granite domes and sheer cliffs were ready-made for lookouts. Constantly at watch from these towering pinnacles, the Apaches could spot their enemies in the valley below.

If you want to explore the stronghold, start by finding the Cochise Indian Trail opposite the information bulletin board. This is an easy, gentle, upward-sloping three-mile hike to the Stronghold Divide and the west side. The west side trail is 1.75 miles downhill. The west side road is very poor, with deep, deep sand. The six-mile hike to the divide and back is a comfortable four hours. The campsites sit at the bottom of the canyon surrounded by 500-foot stone walls. It's simple to imagine Chiricahua Apaches behind the large rock outcrops. B.Y.O. water.

Just down the road from Cochise Stronghold and before the Amerind Foundation are two pistachio farms, **Sehe-ya** (520-826-3718) and **Fistiki Farms**. Sehe-ya, Apache for "our land," offers a hot chili-flavored nut that needs a glass of something to go with it. Fistiki Farms (www.pistachios.com, 800-442-4207), different from Sehe-ya's hot chili variety, makes a

Don't lean on this rock at the Chiricahua National Monument.

PINNACLE BALANCED ROCK

southwestern blend which is more flavorful. The recipe is a closely guarded secret. Both farms offer tastes of their flavored pistachios.

The **Amerind Foundation** (www.amerind.org, 520-586-3666), a contraction for American Indian, established by William S. Fulton in 1937, is located on the west side of Cochise Stronghold. Internationally acclaimed as an archeological research facility and museum, Amerind focuses on the study of Native American Indian culture and history. The museum houses one of the finest privately maintained ethnological collections in the United States. The archeological exhibitions provide glimpses into the past with objects representative of cultures in the Southwest and Mexico. It's a stealthy trip back to Geronimo's hideout from here.

Appendix Elements, My Dear Watson

In this world, it is best to be self-reliant. Plan and prepare.

ATTITUDES IN ALTITUDE

Climbing too fast from plains to mountains can cause altitude sickness. Although minor, who wants headaches and fatigue dogging them for vacations? A couple of suggestions to minimize the chances;

1) Spend a night or two at 5,000 feet before going to 10,000. It gives the body time to adjust.

2) Drink two or three times as much water as normal to replenish the water lost in the normally dry alpine air.

3) Reduce salt, alcohol, and caffeine intake. All of these increase the severity of altitude sickness.

4) Throttle back heavy physical exercise to moderate levels.

5) Use sunscreens. At high altitudes, the ultraviolet rays burn more quickly. Besides, who looks good when their lips, nose, and forehead are blistered and red?

The La Sal Mountains can be viewed from up high.

6) Seek help and lower the altitude if headache and/or nausea persist for more than two days.

HEAT STRESS DISORDERS, OR "SOME LIKE IT TOO HOT"

Drink water before you are thirsty and at least a gallon a day in the desert. Water in the canteen serves no purpose.

HEAT CRAMPS

Symptoms: painful muscle cramps caused by failure to replace lost salt.

Treatment: drink lightly salted water, lemonade, tomato juice, or Gatorade. Stretch cramped muscle.

HEAT EXHAUSTION

Symptoms: very pale face, nausea, cool, moist skin, headache, cramps caused by failure to replace lost bodily fluids.

Treatment: find shade, drink water, eat food, cool the body, and rest.

HEAT STROKE

Symptoms: flushed and red face, hot, dry skin, weak and rapid pulse, high temperature, inability to cope, unconsciousness caused by total collapse of the body's temperature regulating mechanisms. Victim is in extreme danger of brain damage and death.

Treatment: find shade, cool victim immediately with water and fan rapidly to increase evaporative cooling, seek help.

HYPOTHERMIA, OR "BABY IT'S COLD INSIDE"

Symptoms: uncontrolled shivering, poor muscle control, careless attitude, caused by exhaustion and exposure to cold, wet, windy weather. This can happen any season in the higher elevations.

Treatment: put on dry clothes, give warm fluids and warm body contact with another person, protect from wind, rain, and cold. Hypothermia can occur when temperatures are as warm as 50 degrees Fahrenheit.

FLASHING . . . FLOODS

Thunderstorms are frequent and violent. When you notice water changing from clear to muddy, hear a roar from up-canyon, or see stronger currents or quickly rising water, a flash flood is coming. It does not have to be raining on you for you to get caught. Never try to beat a flood! Move to higher ground until the water levels subside.

WHAT KIND OF WEATHER WILL YOU HAVE

To give you a sense of the kind of weather to expect on your travels we've listed some cities in the region with their average high and low seasonal temperatures in Fahrenheit, relative humidity, and precipitation in inches.

City (Altitude)	Jan–Mar	April–June	July–Sept	Oct–Dec
Flagstaff (7,000 feet)	44/15, 50%, 6	66/20, 35%, 4	80/40, 32%, 6	73/22, 39%, 5
Phoenix (1,107 feet)	67/39, 48%, 2	84/52, 31%, 1	103/74, 30%, 2	87/57, 39%, 2
Tucson (2,555 feet)	65/39, 46%, 2	81/50, 30%, 1	97/71, 38%, 5	83/56, 40%, 2
Yuma (194 feet)	74/43, 43%, 1	94/50, 33%, 1	107/71, 35%, 1	101/50, 41%, 1
Co. Springs (6,170 feet)	45/16, 51%, 2	69/24, 49%, 7	85/52, 53%, 6	75/25, 50%, 3
Denver (5,332 feet)	45/18, 57%, 2	60/34, 53%, 6	84/56, 52%, 5	66/37, 53%, 3
Gr. Junction (4,843 feet)	44/16, 58%, 2	75/39, 34%, 2	93/56, 27%, 2	81/29, 40%, 3
Las Vegas (2,180 feet)	58/34, 42%, 1	78/50, 27%, 1	101/72, 22%, 1	80/53, 30%, 1
Albuquerque (5,314 feet)	49/25, 54%, 1	70/41, 36%, 1	90/63, 41%, 3	71/44, 48%, 2
Salt Lake City (4,227 feet)	40/21, 73%, 4	62/36, 54%, 5	88/57, 63%, 3	65/39, 67%, 3
Avg. high (°F)/Avg. low (°F), Rel. humidity (%), total precip. (inches)				

WHEN LIGHTNING STRIKES

If caught above timberline in a thunderstorm, get off the ridges and try to drop quickly in elevation. If that's not possible, put distance between you and metal objects. Yes, there is still metal in the new steeds.

If in timber, seek shelter in a clump of small trees. Get away from tall ones; avoid hilltops. If caught in the open with only a few trees around, separate yourself from the steed and crouch—don't lie down—twice the distance from the tree as the tree is high. Maintain as little contact with the ground as possible. If with a group, spread out.

If your hair stands on end, sparks start coming off a sharp object, or you hear a humming or crackling sound in rocks, lightning is about to strike. Drop to your knees, place hands on knees, bend your head forward and curl up your body to present the smallest target. No, don't kiss your ass good-bye.

If someone is struck, the immediate danger is cardiac arrest. They do not carry the charge—it is safe to touch them. If necessary, perform CPR and treat for burns until help arrives.

Index

About the Author

Marty Berke writes motorcycle travel guides out of a lifelong love of the open road. A resident of Mexico Beach, Florida, he caught the two-wheeled touring bug with his first Schwinn, and graduated to the motorized species not long afterward with a 1955 Vespa, a driver's license, and a $50 IOU to Mom.

After graduating from C.W. Post College with a degree in economics, Marty joined the international division of a large high-tech corporation and spent fifteen years pursuing his hobby—touring—while setting up new businesses and marketing programs throughout Europe, the Americas, the South Pacific, and Asia.

Marty, an MSF instructor, now focuses on finding good roads all over the world and new ways to share them with you. Check out his book *Motorcycle Journeys Through the New England*, if your plans take you to that palace of riding pleasure.

Here's Marty and Ava Pauline, the third generation of Berke Biker Babes. (Photo by Tara Maric, Ava's Mom)